INSTRUCTIONS

FOR

Cutting out Apparel for the Poor;

Principally intended for the Affiftance of the

PATRONESSES of SUNDAY SCHOOLS,

And other CHARITABLE INSTITUTIONS

But USEFUL in all FAMILIES.

●

CONTAINING

Patterns, Directions, and Calculations, whereby the moft Inexperienced may readily buy the Materials, cut out and value each Article of Cloathing of every Size, without the leaft Difficulty, and with the greateft Exactnefs:

With a PREFACE,

Containing a Plan for affifting the Parents of poor Children belonging to SUNDAY SCHOOLS, to clothe them; and other ufeful Obfervations.

———

Publifhed for the Benefit of the

SUNDAY SCHOOL CHILDREN

At *HERTINGFORDBURY,*

In the County of *HERTFORD;*

Where the above Plan has been found to be the beft Encouragement to the Parents to fend their Children to the Sunday School, and at the fame Time the beft Source of Employment for the Schools of Induftry.

═══════

LONDON:

Sold by J. WALTER, Charing Crofs.

M,DCC,LXXXIX.

PREFACE.

THE following little tract has been haftily compiled from a collection of memorandums made for private convenience, to fave the trouble of repeated calculation and contrivance every time there was occafion to furnifh any of the articles hereafter fpecified. Having been found of fingular fervice to this purpofe, and being much fought for by feveral friends, and others concerned in Charitable Inftitutions, however willingly and gladly a convenience of fo trifling a nature was communicated, the tranfcribing and preparing the feveral heads of information was found to break in fo much upon other neceffary occupations and employments, that the idea prefented itfelf of committing a few copies to the prefs, principally for the accommodation of friends; with which view therefore, the materials were put into the prefent form. It afterwards occurred, that if a larger number fhould happen to be wanted, a profit might enfue from a fale of the remainder, which would encreafe the fund of the little Eftablifhments that firft gave rife to the plan itfelf; and to which purpofe any profit that may arife will be faithfully appropriated.

The Eftablifhments above mentioned are, two Sunday Schools, and two Day Schools, or what are generally termed, Schools of Induftry. So much has been ably written in recommendation of thefe Inftitutions, that inferior attempts would be ufelefs. But the difficulty has been to devife a permanent inducement to Parents to fend their Children

to

to the former of thefe ufeful Seminaries, without breaking in too much upon the funds fub-
fcribed for their eftablifhment, by donations of
money or cloathing, which in the end have
been found too often to defeat the falutary
purpofe for which they were intended. The
plan that is now fubmitted to the generous
Benefactors of the Infant Poor, is to appro-
priate a fmall part only of the Sunday School
Fund towards *affifting* the Parents to clothe
their Children; and the affiftance that has
been found fully adequate to that purpofe is,
an allowance of *one fourth* part only of the
price of every article of cloathing at the prime
coft of the materials after the fame has been
made up by the girls at the Day School, or
School of Induftry. This allowance, though
at firft fight it may appear to be an advantage
of only 25 *per cent.* will, upon the loweft
calculation, be found to produce a faving in
fact of 50 *per cent.* and in fome articles con-
fiderably more.

It is to be obferved however, that the
above faving of 50 *per cent.* can only take
place where there is a School of Induftry,
upon a plan fimilar to that eftablifhed in the
Parifh of *Hertingfordbury.* At this School
of Induftry the materials for work are all
found by the Sunday School Fund. The
parents are at the fole expence of teaching
the children; viz. 3 *d. per* week for each
fcholar; and the work, when finifhed, is
brought home to the warehoufe of the Charity Fund, to be purchafed at the prime coft
of the materials, deducting the allowance of
one fourth before mentioned. The parents
of

of the child or children working each article have the preference of buying it. The *making* of each article being *gratis*, may fairly be eftimated at 15 *per cent*. which added to 20 *per cent*. gained upon the purchafe of the materials wholefale, makes 35 *per cent*. and the allowance of a fourth part of the price being nearly 20 *per cent*. more, makes altogether at leaft a faving of 50 *per cent*.

A condition annexed to this regulation is, that no parent can have the benefit of it whofe child does not belong to the Sunday School, from whence three material advantages have been found to refult: 1ft. It induces the parents to permit, and even to be anxious for their children to attend the Sunday School. 2dly. It materially affifts the parents in providing their children with decent cloathing, which removes the difficulty that has arifen in moft places in refpect of the appearance of the Sunday School Children; and inftead of encouraging idlenefs, which, as has been before obferved, is too often the cafe with *donations* of money or cloathing, it is a fpur to induftry. A little money thus appropriated is of fo extenfive an affiftance, that even if the above objection did not lie to partial Benefactions of cloathing to particular children, the fame fum neceffary to that purpofe will be found of infinitely more benefit, if fo applied, as will appear from the fpecimen here fubjoined, which is, with diffidence, fubmitted to the confideration of thofe who at prefent affift the Sunday School Fund with fuch kind Donations.

A LIST

A LIST of Apparel purchased in one Year by the Parents for the Children belonging to the Sunday School at *Hertingfordbury*, allowing them One Fourth of the Price of each Article at Prime Cost, after being made up by the Girls belonging to the School of Industry.

Article	Cost			Sold at			Expence to the Charity		
	l.	s.	d.	l.	s.	d.	l.	s.	d.
36 Aprons	2	4	9½	1	13	7¼	0	11	2¼
49 Caps	0	18	8¼	0	14	0¼	0	4	8
11 Gowns	2	13	8	2	0	3	0	13	5
19 Handkerchiefs	1	2	7	0	16	11¼	0	5	7¾
9 Petticoats	0	13	1	0	9	9¾	0	3	3¼
44 Shifts	3	8	10½	2	11	8	0	17	2½
39 Shirts	3	12	3½	2	14	2	0	18	0¾
48 Pair of Stockings	2	14	7½	2	0	11¾	0	13	7¾
6 Tippets	0	2	0	0	1	6	0	0	6
32 Hats *	3	0	6	2	5	4½	0	15	1½
69 Pair of Shoes *	10	14	6	8	0	10½	2	13	7½
2 Suits of Boys Cloaths, Waistcoats *, &c.	2	8	0	1	16	0	0	12	0
Totals, Cost, Sold at, and Expence to the Charity,	33	13	7½	25	5	2¾	8	8	4¾

N. B. The articles marked thus * were purchased at the shops, and the fourth part of the price deducted.

Laſtly. It provides the Day School for the Girls, or School of Induſtry, with conſtant materials for teaching them to work, which the poverty of moſt of the parents renders it impoſſible for them otherwiſe to have. As the great object with reſpect to the poorer ſort of girls is, to bring them up with the ability to make good ſervants, and uſeful mothers to families of their own, the regulation in the Schools alluded to, is not only to teach them knitting and plain-work, but to inſtruct them in the neceſſary article of *mending* their own things : For this purpoſe, and for the greater eaſe of the Schoolmiſtreſs, a week is allotted to each employment; viz. one week for knitting, the next week for plain-work, and the third week the parents are directed to ſend the linen belonging to themſelves and families to be mended and repaired ; and the fourth week the children return to knitting again.

It may be proper here to mention another mode of aſſiſtance greatly beneficial to the Poor, which, though it has not the merit of novelty to recommend it, has a claim to notice from long experience of its utility; namely, that moſt acceptable one of providing for the neceſſities of poor Lying-in Women. Many public charities are eſtabliſhed in *London* with this benevolent view, but experience authoriſes the declaration, that none is more acceptable and ſalutary than that of ſupplying the neceſſary and comfortable apparel for the mother and child at that expenſive period. The quantity ſpe-

cified

cified in the enfuing pages is fufficient, which it is recommended fhould be lent for the month, and a week more allowed to return the fet clean and in order, as it was received. This faves the expence of preparation to the poor family, perhaps the whole of which is afterwards laid by ufelefs for a length of time. A little attention to the purchafe of the different articles makes the expence trifling; and it is needlefs to obferve, that three or four fets will, under the above regulation, be fufficient for a Parifh of confiderable extent. This benefit may be ftill further encreafed, where convenient, by a few things flightly put together of any old materials, if only a few caps or fhirts, to give to fuch parents as are moft deferving, when they return the fet that has been lent them. For this purpofe there will be found a pattern of a night cap or boy's cap in Pl. XIII, Fig. 2, and of a girl's cap Fig. 3, which require lefs work than the patterns of thofe which are lent to them during the month.

In refpect of thefe Inftitutions, there are various publications which point out fome fimilar benefits, but the moft diligent enquiry has not difcovered one which has minutely fpecified *the mode* of furnifhing Apparel for the poor with the beft œconomy, or which contain any thing more on the fubject than a calculation of general expence, moft commonly exceeding what is neceffary, and without any direction how to keep even that expence within the bounds prefcribed, or to enable any body to purchafe the materials to the beft advantage, and proceed to the

ufe

ufe of them, without confulting others, whofe particular bufinefs it may have been, how to cut them out : of courfe, leaving every body to the inconvenience of forming their own plans, patterns, and calculations, and to make trials of each. The directions in the enfuing Tract are prefented as having been fuccefsful in themfelves, though, no doubt, open to the improvement of further experiment.

Much repetition will be found in the various inftructions, which neceffarily arifes from every part of each different article requiring the fame terms of length, width, breadth, &c. to defcribe it. It is eafy to defcribe the length or breadth of any thing; but where different foldings and doublings are required to be expreffed to make a thing which admits of *no pattern*, it is very difficult for words to render it intelligible. For the fake of exactnefs in the admeafurement, a fcale has been introduced in Pl. IV, the extent of which is one quarter of a yard; and the fmaller divifions of nail, half nail, and inch, are more accurately marked than in the common meafures made ufe of. Upon the whole, although there may be particular articles that will, perhaps, require fome little confideration to comprehend, and the defcription of which may appear very obfcure on a curfory view, yet it is conceived that, with the commodity in the hand, and an attention to each meafure and direction as they follow each other, the intended object will not fail to be gained, almoft without any previous knowledge on the fubject.

For

For further information on the fubject of purchafing all the commodities neceffary to carry into execution charitable purpofes of this kind, and for the convenience particularly of thofe who refide in the country, and may have occafion to fend their orders in writing, a felection and defcription of each article has been made from the work, and annexed; that at one view they may be known, and ordered from the fhops without trouble, or the neceffity of feeking information at the time.

Since the foregoing pages were put together it occurred, that the means fo fuccefsfully practifed of affifting the poor in the article of cloathing, might occafionally, and in fevere feafons, be applied towards the reduction of the heavy expence of *provifions*; accordingly, in the late fevere froft, the feveral families in the Parifh of *Hertingfordbury* before-mentioned, to the amount of eighty in number, were fent to, and enquiry made as to the quantity of bread each particular family confumed in a week. That being afcertained, and the price of bread and flour being at that time $7\frac{1}{4}d$. *per* quartern loaf, they were given to underftand, that for every quartern loaf, or for every quarter of flour that they confumed, they would have an allowance of $2d$. The greater part of the parifh purchafe flour and bake their own bread. The mode by which this charity was conducted is as follows: Weekly Tickets were made out, containing the name of every family, the number of quartern loaves or quarterns

of

of flour each family confumed, and the deduction to be allowed on the refpective quantities at the rate of 2 *d. per* quartern; for inftance, " *A. B.* and family confume " twelve quarterns *per* week, allow 2 *s.*"—— This done, notice was given to the different mealmen and bakers with whom each family dealt, to receive the above ticket figned by the Donor, as fo much money on behalf of the perfon who brought it, with directions to fend it to the Donor as a check to be compared with the bill for the different allowances to each family. By this Plan the poor of the parifh were fupplied for fix weeks with bread at $5\frac{1}{4}$ *d. per* quartern loaf, and flour proportionably lefs, at the very fmall expence of three guineas and an half *per* week, which fum would have been of little fervice amongft fo many as eighty families, had it been diftributed in loaves. This further advantage accrued, that by means of the whole fix weeks allowance being advanced at a time, moft of the families were enabled to purchafe a fack, or half a fack of flour at once; in which quantity they bought it at the wholefale price, and thereby made an additional faving of nearly 20 *per cent.* The gratitude and thankfulnefs of the poor individuals thus relieved, is an additional proof how much preferable an affiftance of this fort is to giving away fo much bread, or meat, or broth, with the quality of, or with the manner of doing which, they are apt too often to be diffatisfied. How frequently has it been found, that donations of bread, made of the moft wholefome

pure

pure flour, have been neglected and abfo-
lutely refufed by the poor from mere igno-
rance, becaufe it was not what they call
" *white bread.*"   So, in all probability,
would this affiftance have been rejected, if,
inftead of each family being left at liberty to
purchafe from their own baker or mealman,
they had been directed to buy the flour or
bread of one particular baker only, which cer-
tainly would have faved the Donor a great deal
of trouble; for whether from whim and ca-
price, or to whatever other caufe owing, it is
a fact, that in the above Parifh there are no lefs
than fourteen different perfons who furnifh
the refpective families with flour and bread:
it was neceffary therefore to fend to every one
of thofe perfons the notice above mentioned.
But by indulging each family in the liberty to
purchafe of their own tradefman, all was
harmony, gratitude, and content.   The great
fecret of fuccefs in thefe refpects, feems to be
a little attention to the particularities of the
lower rank of people, and to make them feel,
as little as poffible, their own dependance in
the obligation you confer upon them.

IN-

INSTRUCTIONS

FOR

Cutting out Apparel for the Poor *.

Directions for reducing the Price of the Materials.

THE method of reducing the different articles hereafter mentioned to the low prices specified, is by purchasing each commodity wholesale, by which there is a considerable saving in the prime cost, besides an additional gain in the quantity charged, which is very material to be attended to. For instance, in the sale of a piece of *Irish* cloth, it is usual for the wholesale trader to charge the piece at 25 yards only, which, in general, will run 26 yards; consequently a piece charged as above, as containing 25 yards, and bought at 1 s. 1 d. a yard, may be sold to the poor at 1 s. $0\frac{1}{2}$ d. a yard. For

	s.	d.	l.	s.	d.
25 yards at 1 :	1	=	1 :	7 :	1
26 yards at 1 :	$0\frac{1}{2}$	=	1 :	7 :	1

---

* N. B. Although this work is intended more immediately for this purpose, yet it is apprehended the directions for cutting out many of the articles, especially shirts and shifts, may be equally useful in all families, and particularly where there are a number of children requiring a variety of sizes. For, provided the widths of the cloths correspond, the quality being fine or coarse makes no difference in any thing, but in the advance on the price.

B

Directions for calculating the Price of the Articles.

In calculating the price of any article where a fraction arifes, the following method has been purfued; viz. Suppofe the value of any article to be fold amounts to 2 *s.* $7\frac{3}{4}$ *d.* it is charged to the purchafer at 2 *s.* 8 *d.* So alfo in deducting the allowance of one fourth upon the price, fuppofe the price were 2 *s.* $8\frac{1}{2}$ *d.* call one fourth 8 *d.* and the actual price will be 2 *s.* $0\frac{1}{2}$ *d.* Again, where tapes are ufed, fuch an allowance is to be made in addition to the fmall fum charged for them, as may make the fum at which the article is to be fold, even money; for inftance, if in the value calculated there is an odd halfpenny, it is charged a penny. The reafon of placing this furcharge to the expence of the purchafer, is to make a fuf-ficient allowance for materials, fuch as thread, needles, fhirt buttons, &c. of which the exact quantity that will be ufed in making up the different articles cannot be particularly fpecified. This method alfo provides for any accidental lofs or wafte that may arife on cutting out the various com-modities.

8

CLOATHING for GIRLS;

With One Fourth of the Price
deducted.

APRONS. Made of Check at 12 *d.* a yard, exactly three quarters wide. Tape at 6¾ *d.* the piece, containing 19 yards and a quarter; or striped tape at 9*d.* the piece, containing 24 yards.

APRON, N° 1, or longeft.

	s.	*d.*
Two yards of check — —	2	0
Two yards of tape, and thread —	0	1
Price —	2	1
Deduct a 4th —	0	6¼
Sold at —	1	7

APRON, N° 2, or fecond fize.

	s.	*d.*
One yard and a half — —	1	6
One yard and a half of tape, and thread	0	1
Price —	1	7
Deduct a 4th —	0	4¾
Sold at —	1	2½

APRON, N° 3, or third fize.

	s.	*d.*
Three quarters and a half — —	0	10½
One yard and a quarter of tape, and thread	0	0½
Price —	0	11
Deduct a 4th —	0	2¾
Sold at —	0	8½

APRON, N° 1. *How cut out.*

Two yards of check will make one apron, doubled acrofs, and cut one breadth out of the other for the flope; which makes the apron a yard and near half a quarter long. Two yards of tape for the binding.

   N. B. To make the proper flope, meafure a yard and three quarters of a nail from each end, on the contrary fides of the check, and crofs it to each pin. This makes the flope a nail and a half deep.

APRON, N° 2. *How cut out.*

Three yards make two aprons, divided in three breadths, and one breadth fplit. A breadth and a half in each apron, the floping about a nail deep, leaving two or three inches ftrait at the corners of the apron. Bound with the floping. A yard and a half of tape cut in half, and fewed to the ends of the binding, for the ftrings.

APRON, N° 3. *How cut out.*

One breadth in the apron, three quarters and a half long. The flope, &c. the fame as N° 2. A yard and a quarter of tape for the ftrings.

A P R O N S.

APRON, N° 4, or fourth size.

		s.		d.
Three quarters and a fourth of a quarter		o	:	9¾
Tape and thread — —		o	:	o¾
Price —		o	:	10½
Deduct a 4ᵗʰ —		o	:	2½
Sold at —		o	:	8

APRON, N° 5, or fifth size.

		s.		d.
Half a yard, half a quarter, and a fourth of a quarter — —		o	:	8¼
Tape and thread — —		o	:	o¾
Price —		o	:	9
Deduct a 4ᵗʰ —		o	:	2¼
Sold at —		o	:	7

APRON, N° 6, or smallest size.

		s.		d.
Half a yard, and the fourth of a quarter		o	:	6¾
Tape and thread — —		o	:	o¾
Price —		o	:	7½
Deduct a 4ᵗʰ —		o	:	1¾
Sold at —		o	:	6

APRON, N° 4. *How cut out.*

Three quarters long, with a bib. A quarter of a yard (the breadth doubled in four) makes four bibs, the corners a little floped off at the bottom to anfwer the flope of the apron in fetting it on. Bound with the floping, and one yard of tape for the ftrings.

APRON, N° 5. *How cut out.*

Half a yard, and half a quarter long: with a bib, the fame as N° 4, bound with the floping of the apron, and one yard of tape for the ftrings.

APRON, N° 6. *How cut out.*

Half a yard long: with a bib, the fame as N° 4 and 5, bound with the floping of the apron, and one yard of tape for the ftrings.

B 4

BONNETS. Made of black Durant at 15 d. a yard, called yard wide, but meafures three quarters and half a nail only. Pafteboard 2½ d. a fheet. Quality fhoe binding 2 s. the piece, containing 32 yards. Black thread.

BONNET, N° 1, largeft.

	s.	d.
Half a yard, and half a quarter of ftuff	0 :	9¼
The third of a fheet of pafteboard —	0 :	0¾
Binding and thread — —	0 :	1
Price —	0 :	11
Deduct a 4th —	0 :	2¾
Sold at —	0 :	8½

BONNET, N° 2, fmalleft.

	s.	d.
One quarter of a yard, one half quarter, and one nail of ftuff — —	0 :	6½
One quarter of a fheet of pafteboard —	0 :	0½
Binding and thread — —	0 :	1
Price —	0 :	8
Deduct a 4th —	0 :	2
Sold at —	0 :	6

A binder of the fame may be added to thefe bonnets, herring-boned at the edges with blue worfted, which will add one penny to the price.

BONNET, Nº 1. *How cut out.*

One yard and a nail make one front and a half, and two cauls. The breadth doubled in three, will be the width of the pattern of the front, Plate I, Fig. 1. The remainder will be the proper width for the cauls; the felvedge at the bottom, the length of two in the breadth of the ftuff, the ends at the top rounded, and a cafe added (for the ftring) at the bottom, which comes out of the floping of the fronts. One fheet of pafteboard makes three fronts, in the length. Three quarters of a yard of black binding for the ftrings. A hole made in the caul to tie behind.

N. B. The pafteboard muft be cut exactly the fize of the pattern, and the ftuff large enough to turn over.

BONNET, Nº 2. *How cut out.*

Three quarters, half a quarter and a nail, make two bonnets. The breadth makes four widths (cut one out of the other) of the Pattern, Plate I, Fig. 2, which compleats two fronts. The remainder is the proper width for the cauls, one quarter and a half, and one nail wide; the felvedge at the bottom, the length of two in the breadth of the ftuff, and a broad hem for the cafe. One fheet of pafteboard makes four fronts, three in the width, and one off of the end. Three quarters of a yard of black binding for the ftrings; a hole in the caul to tie behind.

N. B. The cover of the front is tacked over the edge of the pafteboard, the caul plaited on the infide of the pafteboard, the hem even with the end, and then the lining run in.

CAPS. Made of *Irish* Cloth at 15 *d. per* yard, runs yard wide all but an inch. And of $\frac{7}{8}$ wide *Irish*, at 12 *d. per* yard, runs three quarters and half quarter all but about an inch. *Hanover* lace at 1 *s.* 4$\frac{1}{2}$ *d.* the piece, ditto at 1 *s.* each containing 9 yards. Tape 3$\frac{1}{2}$ *d.* the piece, 18 yards and a half; and ditto at 6$\frac{1}{4}$ *d.* the piece, 19 yards and a quarter in the piece.

CAP, N° 1, or largest size, $\frac{7}{8}$ *Irish*, 12 *d. per* yard.

	s.	*d.*
One quarter of a yard of *Irish* — —	0 :	3
One yard of *Hanover* lace — —	0 :	2$\frac{1}{2}$
Tape and thread — — —	0 :	0$\frac{1}{2}$
Price —	0 :	6
Deduct a 4th —	0 :	1$\frac{1}{2}$
Sold at —	0 :	4$\frac{1}{2}$

CAP, N° 2, or second size, yard wide, at 15 *d.*

	s.	*d.*
A sixth of a yard — — —	0 :	2$\frac{1}{2}$
Three quarters and a half of *Hanover* lace	0 :	2$\frac{1}{4}$
Tape and thread — — —	0 :	0$\frac{1}{2}$
Price —	0 :	5$\frac{1}{4}$
Deduct a 4th —	0 :	1$\frac{1}{4}$
Sold at —	0 :	4

CAP, N° 3, or smallest size, yard wide, at 15 *d.*

	s.	*d.*
Half a quarter of a yard — —	0 :	1$\frac{3}{4}$
Three quarters of a yard of *Hanover* lace	0 :	1$\frac{1}{4}$
Tape and thread — —	0 :	0$\frac{1}{2}$
Price —	0 :	3$\frac{1}{2}$
Deduct a 4th —	0 :	0$\frac{3}{4}$
Sold at —	0 :	3

CAP, N° 1. *How cut out.*

Four yards all but one nail and a half make sixteen caps and half a head-piece. The breadth doubled in half, and then in three, makes the proper width for the head-pieces; therefore four lengths of the half head-piece, Pattern Pl. II, Fig. 1, make twelve. The width of a head-piece taken off the side of the rest of the cloth, makes in length four head-pieces and a half, and the remainder of the cloth makes the sixteen cauls. The width of two in the width, and the length of eight in the length, Pattern Pl. III, Fig. 1. One yard of *Hanover* lace. One yard and a quarter of tape, at $3\frac{1}{2}$ *d.* the piece.

CAP, N° 2. *How cut out.*

A yard and half a quarter make six cauls, and eight head-pieces. The breadth doubled in three makes the width of the caul, Pattern Pl. III, Fig. 2. two lengths of the caul therefore make six, being three double. The remainder doubled the width in four, makes two head-pieces, Pattern Pl. II, Fig. 2, in width, and two lengths of the half head-piece, which is eight in all. Three quarters and a half of *Hanover* lace. One yard and half a quarter of tape of the same breadth as N° 1.

N. B. Four yards will make exactly two dozen caps.

CAP, N° 3. *How cut out.*

One quarter of a yard makes two. The width doubled in four, the selvedge to the face, Pattern Pl. IV, Fig. 1. Three quarters of a yard of *Hanover* lace. One yard of tape, at $6\frac{3}{4}$ *d.* the piece.

N. B. One piece of *Hanover* lace trims twelve caps of this size.

CLOAKS. Made of grey Duffeild, or coating, at 2 *s. per* yard, called yard wide, but meafures three quarters and half a quarter only. Narrow worfted ferret for binding, at 11 *d.* the piece, containing 30 yards. Ditto broader for ftrings, at 20 *d.* the piece, containing 32 yards and three quarters. Grey thread, at 3 *s. per* pound.

CLOAK, N° 1, or largeft fize.

	l.	s.	d.
One yard, three quarters and a half of Duffeild — —	0 :	3 :	9
Binding and thread — —	0 :	0 :	3
Price —	0 :	4 :	0
Deduct a 4th —	0 :	1 :	0
Sold at —	0 :	3 :	0

CLOAK, N° 1. *How cut out.*

One yard, three quarters, and half a quarter make one. A yard and a half in the width of the cloak, the felvedges at the top and bottom. A piece cut about an inch from the bottom of the front of the cloak floping off (towards the hind part) to form the elbows. The front of the cloak is floped from the top by taking the corners off, a nail and a quarter deep (along the felvedge,) and flanting to a point towards the middle of the front of the cloak, a quarter and a half in length, from the felvedge. A piece the
fhape

shape of a gore to be added to the strait part of the front of the cloak, to form the slope to the bottom. A fourth of the breadth of the cloth, (the length of half a yard all but a nail, cut acrofs like gores, only quite to a point,) will make thefe two pieces; the remainder of the width of the cloth, is the depth for two hoods, one quarter and a nail deep each. They muft be three quarters wide all but one nail, the felvedge round the face. The hood will require a flope from the back of the neck about three quarters of a nail deep, flanted to a point to the corners; and another about a nail deep floping about half way up the back of the hood, alfo to a point, leaving nearly a quarter and a half for the crown. The hoods will be about half a yard in width to fet on the collar, which comes out of the neck of the cloak; viz. The neck floped out a nail and three quarters deep behind, beginning one nail deep at the front, which leaves the cloak behind three quarters long. This piece makes the collar, infide and out, a nail wide, and half a yard and half a nail long; the ends floped a little to the top. Two yards and a quarter, and three nails of narrow binding will bind the front of the cloak and hood, and the ends of the collar infide and out. A yard and half a quarter of broader binding to run in the neck, and three quarters of ditto may be added for two ftrings to be fixed on each fide, to tie acrofs the breaft.

N. B. In making thefe cloaks the raw edges may be fewed together and preffed down with an iron.

CLOAKS.

CLOAK, N° 2, or second size.

	s.	d.
One yard, one quarter, and half a quarter	2	9
Binding and thread — —	0	3
Price —	3	0
Deduct a 4th —	0	9
Sold at —	2	3

CLOAK, N° 3, or smallest size.

	s.	d.
One yard and half a quarter —	2	3
Binding and thread — —	0	3
Price —	2	6
Deduct a 4th —	0	$7\frac{1}{2}$
Sold at —	1	11

CLOAKS, N° 2, and 3. *How cut out.*

One yard and a quarter in the width of each. The three fizes are cut half a quarter fhorter than each other behind. Two hoods for N° 3, will come from the remainder in the width of the breadth left at the top of N° 2. They will be a full quarter deep, and half a yard and half a quarter wide; require a fmall hollow in the neck, and a little flope from the crown to the neck behind. This piece will alfo be wide enough for the front gores to either fize; viz. Two, cut one out of the other in the width, the felvedge down the fide. The fame piece remaining in cutting out the cloak N° 3, will make a hood and a half, in the length, for the cloak N° 2, the felvedge down the face; the half hoods will join at the top very well, by fewing the raw edges to-gether. Thefe hoods will be a quarter and near a nail deep, and half a yard and a quarter wide. The collars (the three fizes a quarter of a nail fhorter than each other) will come out of the re-maining pieces, but if neceffary to cut fome out of a frefh quantity, the width of the cloth will make two in length, of the fmalleft fize. Near the fame quantity of binding and thread as allowed for N° 1.

N. B. Seventy-two yards of grey Duffeild, cut out according to the above directions, one with another, make fifty cloaks; viz.

    10 Cloaks N° 1, or largeft fize;
    25 Ditto N° 2, or fecond fize;
    15 Ditto N° 3, or fmalleft fize.

    ——
    50
    ——

GOWNS.

May be made of stuff or grogram. The former is the beft for children. There are fuch a variety of widths and prices, that it is not eafy to afcertain the value, or quantity for the different fizes of gowns; or to give any directions about the larger fizes, as they are generally made, (even amongft the poor people,) by fome whofe particular employment it is.

A few memorandums only therefore are added of the different quantities that have been required, and the pattern and directions for cutting out a fmall gown; which might be made larger upon the fame plan. The materials moft commonly ufed are;

Grograms, at 12 d. per yard, called yard wide, but meafure three quarters, one nail, and a half only.

Stuffs at 7 d. 7½ d. and 8 d. per yard, half yard wide, 29½ yards in the piece.

Stuff called *Leeds Manchefter*, at 8 d. per yard, half yard wide.

Linfey woolfeys at 11 d. per yard, called yard wide, but meafure three quarters and half quarter only *.

Body-lining, *Scotch* cloth at 9 d. per yard, runs three quarters and one nail wide.

Coloured threads at 3 s. and finer ditto at 4 s. per pound.

---

* *N. B.* The whole pieces of thefe articles vary in the number of yards that they contain, but there is always an advantage of over meafure in purchafing the whole piece.

GOWNS.

GOWN, Nº 1, or largest size.

	s.	d.
Seven yards of stuff, at 7 *d. per* yard —	4 :	1
One yard of body-lining, at 9 *d. per* yard	0 :	9
Thread — — —	0 :	1
Price —	4 :	10
Deduct a 4th —	1 :	2½
Sold at —	3 :	7½

GOWN, Nº 2, or second size.

	s.	d.
Four yards of grogram, at 12 *d. per* yard	4 :	0
Three quarters of a yard of body-lining, at 9 *d. per* yard — —	0 :	6¾
Thread — — —	0 :	1¼
Price —	4 :	8
Deduct a 4th —	1 :	2
Sold at —	3 :	6

GOWN, Nº 3, or third size.

	s.	d.
* Three yards of linsey woolsey striped, at 10¾ *d. per* yard — —	2 :	8½
Three quarters of a yard of body-lining	0 :	6¼
Thread — — —	0 :	0¾
Price —	3 :	4
Deduct a 4th —	0 :	10
Sold at —	2 :	6

* Viz. Two yards and a half in the skirt, the selvedge at the bottom: And the other half yard makes the body and sleeves. *N. B.* The price in this article is reduced to 10¾ *d.* by the over-measure which is gained by purchasing the whole piece.

C

GOWN, N° 4. *How cut out.*

Three yards of ftuff, half a yard wide, at 7 *d.* *per* yard, make the gown. Half a yard and one nail for the body and fleeves. The breadth doubled down the middle and the half body, Pattern, Plate V, Fig. 1, placed with the felvedges at the top. The fhoulder ftraps (Plate V, Fig. 2) out of the flope at the bottom. The reft of the piece makes the fleeves, Pattern Plate VI, Fig. 1, the felvedge at the top. The remainder of the ftuff cut in three breadths for the fkirt, open before, the middle breadth cut about one nail longer than the others, for the flope. The bottom will allow of a broad hem floping at the corners. This gown will generally require a tuck for a child fix or feven years old.

GOWN, N° 4, or fmalleft fize.

	s.	d.
Three yards of ftuff, at 7 *d. per* yard —	1	9
Half a yard of body-lining — —	0	4½
Thread — — —	0	0½
Price —	2	2
Deduct a 4th —	0	6½
Sold at —	1	7½

By allowing half a yard more in the whole quantity, there will be fufficient to make the fkirt whole before.

HANDKERCHIEFS.

Cotton neck handkerchiefs, at 15 d. and 16 d. apiece, a chocolate colour check, three quarters and a half square.

Linen ditto, at 11 d. blue check, three quarters and a half square, all but half a nail.

Ditto, at 6 d. half a yard and half a quarter square.

Pocket handkerchiefs, red and white, at 6 d. apiece.

Ditto ditto, blue check, at 3 d. apiece, a quarter and a half square.

MITTS, and BOYS GLOVES.

Black worsted mitts of various small sizes, at 5 s. a dozen pair.

Ditto of larger sizes, at 8 s. a dozen pair.

Boys grey worsted gloves of various small sizes, at 5 s. a dozen pair.

Ditto larger sizes, at 7 s. a dozen pair.

PETTICOATS. Made of Grogram at 12 d. *per* yard, called yard wide, but measures three quarters and one nail and a half only. And striped Linsey woolsey at 11 d. *per* yard, called yard wide, but measures three quarters and half a quarter only. *Manchester* tape for the binding at 11 d. the piece, containing 29 yards.

PETTICOAT of Grogram, Nº 1, or largest size.

	s.	d.
Three yards -	3	0
Tape and thread -	0	$0\frac{1}{2}$
Price -	3	$0\frac{1}{2}$
Deduct a 4th	0	9
Sold at -	2	$3\frac{1}{2}$

Ditto of Linsey Woolsey.

	s.	d.
Three yards -	2	9
Tape and thread -	0	$0\frac{1}{2}$
Price -	2	$9\frac{1}{2}$
Deduct a 4th	0	8
Sold at -	2	$1\frac{1}{2}$

Petticoat between Nº 1 and Nº 2, of Linsey Woolsey.

	s.	d.
2 yards and a quarter	2	$0\frac{3}{4}$
Tape and thread -	0	$0\frac{3}{4}$
Price -	2	$1\frac{1}{2}$
Deduct a 4th	0	6
Sold at -	1	$7\frac{1}{2}$

Wider, ditto.

	s.	d.
2 yards and a half	2	$3\frac{1}{2}$
Tape and thread -	0	$0\frac{1}{2}$
Price -	2	4
Deduct a 4th	0	7
Sold at -	1	9

PETTICOAT of Grogram, Nº 2, or second size.

	s.	d.
Two yards — — —	2	0
Tape and thread — — —	0	$0\frac{1}{2}$
Price —	2	$0\frac{1}{2}$
Deduct a 4th —	0	6
Sold at —	1	$6\frac{1}{2}$

PETTICOAT of Grogram, Nº 3, or smallest size.

	s.	d.
One yard and a half	1	6
Tape and thread -	0	$0\frac{1}{2}$
Price -	1	$6\frac{1}{2}$
Deduct a 4th	0	$4\frac{1}{2}$
Sold at -	1	2

Ditto, of Linsey Woolsey.

	s.	d.
One yard and a half	1	$4\frac{1}{2}$
Tape and thread -	0	$0\frac{1}{2}$
Price -	1	5
Deduct a 4th	0	4
Sold at -	1	1

PETTICOAT, N° 1. *How cut out.*

Three yards of grogram cut in three breadths, (the front breadth half a nail shorter than the others, to allow for the slope), this makes the petticoat a yard long, and two yards and a quarter and three nails wide.

The linsey woolsey Petticoat of this size will be a nail and a half wider; if it is striped, the stripes will go round.

Two yards and a quarter of linsey woolsey will make a petticoat between this size and the next, the selvedges at the top and bottom. It will be two yards and a quarter wide, and three quarters and half a quarter long. Or if a size rather larger is wanted, the length will allow for the petticoat to be two yards and a half wide. Very little slope. One yard and a half of tape for the binding.

PETTICOAT, N° 2. *How cut out.*

Two yards of grogram, the selvedges at the top and bottom. The petticoat will be two yards wide, and three quarters and one nail and a half long. One yard and a quarter of tape for the binding. Very little slope.

PETTICOAT, N° 3. *How cut out.*

One yard and a half of grogram divided into two breadths, makes the petticoat three quarters long, and one yard and a half and half a quarter wide. The linsey woolsey petticoats of this size will be a nail wider; and if striped, the stripes will go round. One yard of tape for the binding. Very little slope.

C 3

PETTICOATS. Made of Flannel called $\frac{7}{8}$ wide, at 10 *d. per* yard, but meafures three quarters and half nail only ; and ditto called yard-wide at 12 *d.* but meafures three quarters and half only. *Manchefter* tape 7½ *d.* the piece, containing 27 yards.

PETTICOAT, N° 1, or largeft fize, of flannel $\frac{7}{8}$ wide, at 10 *d. per* yard.

		s.	d.
Two yards and a half	— —	2 :	1
Tape and thread	— —	0 :	1
Price	—	2 :	2
Deduct a 4th	—	0 :	6½
Sold at	—	1 :	7½

PETTICOAT, N° 2, or fecond fize.

One yard and three quarters	— —	1 :	5½
Tape and thread	— — —	0 :	1
Price	—	1 :	6½
Deduct a 4th	—	0 :	4½
Sold at	—	1 :	2

PETTICOAT, N° 3, or fmalleft fize.

One yard and a quarter	— —	1 :	0½
Tape and thread	— —	0 :	0½
Price	—	1 :	1
Deduct a 4th	—	0 :	3¼
Sold at	—	0 :	10

FLANNEL PETTICOAT, N° 1. *How cut out.*

Two yards and half, divided into three breadths, the front breadth cut about half a nail shorter than the others, to allow for the slope. The petticoats will be two yards and three quarters wide, and three quarters and a half long. One yard and a half of tape for the binding.

N. B. Fifteen yards will make six.

FLANNEL PETTICOAT, N° 2. *How cut out.*

One yard and three quarters. The selvedge at the top and bottom. Very little slope. The petticoat will be a yard and three quarters wide, and three quarters and half a nail long. A yard and a quarter of tape for the binding.

N. B. Ten yards and a half will make six.

FLANNEL PETTICOAT, N° 3. *How cut out.*

One yard and a quarter divided across, to cut one breadth out of the other, which makes the slope. *N. B.* This cannot be done, except more than one petticoat is cut out at a time, as the flannel for one breadth will be inside outwards. The petticoat will be a yard and a half wide, and half a yard and half a quarter long. One yard and half a quarter of tape for the binding.

N. B. Seven yards and a half will make six.

PETTICOATS made of flannel at 12*d. per* yard, yard wide.

PETTICOAT, N° 1, or largest size.

	s.	d.
Two yards and a quarter — —	2	3
Tape and thread — — —	0	1
Price —	2	4
Deduct a 4th —	0	7
Sold at —	1	9

PETTICOAT, N° 2, or second size.

One yard and a half — —	1	6
Tape and thread — — —	0	1
Price —	1	7
Deduct a 4th —	0	$4\frac{3}{4}$
Sold at —	1	$2\frac{1}{2}$

PETTICOAT, N° 4, * or smallest size.

Half an ell — — —	0	$7\frac{1}{2}$
Tape and thread — — —	0	$0\frac{1}{2}$
Price —	0	8
Deduct a 4th —	0	2
Sold at —	0	6

* *N. B.* There is no petticoat N° 3, of the flannel of this width.

FLANNEL PETTICOAT, N° 1. *How cut out.*

Two yards and a quarter, the felvedge at the top and bottom. The petticoat will be two yards and a quarter wide, and three quarters one nail and a half long. A yard and a half of tape for the binding. Very little flope.

N. B. Thirteen yards and a half will make fix.

FLANNEL PETTICOAT, N° 2. *How cut out.*

One yard and a half divided into two breadths. The petticoat will be three quarters long, and one yard and three quarters wide. A yard and a quarter of tape for the binding. Very little flope.

N. B. Nine yards will make fix.

FLANNEL PETTICOAT, N° 4. *How cut out.*

One ell divided down the middle of the breadth makes two, leaving the blue felvedges on at the bottom of the petticoats. They will be one yard and a quarter wide, and one quarter and near three nails and a half long. A yard and half a quarter of tape for the binding. Very little flope.

N. B. Three yards and three quarters will make fix.

PIN-CLOTHS. Made of Check, at 12 *d.* *per* yard, three quarters wide. Tape 6¼ *d.* the piece.

PIN-CLOTH, N° 1, or largeſt ſize.

	s.	*d.*
Three quarters and a half — —	0 :	10½
Tape and thread — —	0 :	0½
Price —	0 :	11
Deduct a 4ᵗʰ —	0 :	2¾
Sold at —	0 :	8½

PIN-CLOTH, N° 2, or ſmalleſt ſize.

	s.	*d.*
Three quarters of a yard — —	0 :	9
Tape and thread — —	0 :	0½
Price —	0 :	9½
Deduct a 4ᵗʰ —	0 :	2½
Sold at —	0 :	7

PIN-CLOTH, Nº 1. *How cut out.*

One breadth of check, three quarters of a yard, and half a quarter long, open behind. Doubled down the middle, and the back, Pattern Plate VII, Fig. 1, and the bofom, Pattern Plate VII, Fig. 2, cut out as for a bed-gown. The fides doubled to the middle, and a flit cut down for the arm-hole, half a quarter and a nail long. The top of the fhoulder floped from the neck to the arm-hole near half an inch. The arm-hole wears better if it is rounded a little in the back, at the bottom; and a narrow tape put within the hem at the bottom to ftrengthen it, and prevent it from tearing down. Three quarters of a yard of tape for two ftrings fixed at the corners of the neck behind.

PIN-CLOTH, Nº 2. *How cut out.*

The fame as Nº 1, only three quarters of a yard long. Three quarters of a yard of tape for the two ftrings; and the back and bofom not quite fo deep.

N. B. Thefe pin-cloths are fometimes made of thick brown Holland, or a cloth called Duck, which anfwers very well for boys.

SHIFTS. Made of yard wide *Irish*, at 12 *d.* *per* yard, which measures a yard all but one inch.

SHIFT, N° 1*.

	Yds.	Qrs.	Nails.			
Six bodies	10	0	2			
Six pair sleeves	1	2	3			

	Yds.	Qrs.	Nails.		s.	d.
Call it 12 yards	11	3	1	Value 12 : 0		

		s.	d.
Price of each	—	2	0
Deduct a 4th	—	0	6
Sold at	—	1	6

SHIFT, N° 1. *How cut out.*

Eleven yards three quarters and one nail make six shifts. The bodies a yard and half quarter long; a breadth and a half in each. Cut off nine lengths for the bodies, (viz. ten yards and half a quarter) and divide three of them in half. The half breadth to go behind, and two half gores to be taken from the whole breadth to add to it, to make it the same size as the whole breadth, which may easily be done as follows: Double the whole breadth down the middle, pulling the cloth till it will lay even, then double the half breadth in the same manner, and pin it upon the whole breadth, laying the whole sides to each other; then double what appears of the whole breadth, slanting, for two half gores, allowing the narrow part of the gore at the top a nail wide, and measuring it quite

* *N. B.* This size, made half a quarter of a yard longer, is large enough for most women. The addition will add 2 *d.* to the price.

even,

even, ſo that the narrow and broad parts of the
gores at each end may exactly correſpond with
what is left of the part that appears of the whole
breadth from which they are cut. When the half
gores are cut off, turn the broad ends to the bottom of the ſhift, and pin the ſtrait ſide of the
gores to the ſtrait ſides of the half breadth for
behind; which will make the ſhift compleat.
Before you move the ſhift, cut the boſom, Plate
VIII, Fig. 1, and then the back, Plate VIII,
Fig. 2, (which will be conveniently done, as the
ſhift lays doubled right for each); obſerving to
make the gored breadth for the back. The
ſleeves with wriſtbands. Half a yard and a nail
is the length of the two ſleeves, the width of the
Iriſh makes one pair, (a quarter and half, and a
nail wide) taking the wriſtbands out of the middle
of the breadth, two thirds of a half quarter make
a pair of wriſtbands in width, an inch and a half
wide, the length of the two ſleeves makes one
pair, a quarter of a yard and an inch long each.
One yard and a quarter and three nails make ſix
pair of ſleeves. When the piece for the wriſtbands is taken out, divide the remainder in lengths
for two ſleeves, (viz. half a yard and a nail), double
the two ſides to the middle, and then croſs it for
the ſlope, (to cut one ſleeve out of the other),
allowing a nail difference in the length of the front
and the back of the ſleeve. The guſſets out of the
boſom. The piece to bind the ſleeves comes out
of the cutting of the back and the bottom of the
boſom, when the guſſets are cut out. See Patterns, Letters a a a a. Theſe joined together at
the ends, and divided down the middle, are enough.
N. B. It is better to bind the tops of the ſleeves,
and few them to the ſhift, than to gather them in.

 N. B. Two breadths of *Lancaſhire* Dowlas $\frac{7}{8}$
  wide, is equal in width to the ſize of the
  above ſhift, made of yard wide *Iriſh*. The
  gore taken off of one ſide and put on the
  other.

SHIFT, N° 2, or second size.

		Yds.	Qrs.	Nails.
Six bodies	—	8 :	0 :	0
Sleeves	— —	1 :	0 :	0
		9 :	0 :	0	Value	9 : 0

		s.	d.
Price of each	—	1 :	6
Deduct a 4th	—	0 :	$4\frac{1}{2}$
Sold at	— —	1 :	2

SHIFT, N° 3, or third size.

		Yds.	Qrs.	Nails.
Six bodies	—	5 :	1 :	0
Five gores	—	0 :	3 :	2
One ditto, the 5th of a breadth, 3qrs. 2 nails long —		0 :	0 :	$2\frac{1}{2}$
Sleeves	— —	0 :	3 :	$1\frac{1}{2}$
		7 :	0 :	2	Value	7 : $1\frac{1}{2}$

		s.	d.
Price of each	—	1 :	$2\frac{1}{4}$
Deduct a 4th	—	0 :	$3\frac{3}{4}$
Sold at	— —	0 :	11

SHIFT, N° 2. *How cut out.*

Nine yards make six shifts. The bodies one yard long. One whole breadth and the third of a breadth in each. Eight yards make the six bodies, two of the breadths divided into thirds. The shifts cut out the same as N° 1, only allowing the top of the gore a nail and a half wide, instead of one nail. Three sleeves in a breadth, a quarter long. One yard makes six pair, the width of three in the width, and the length of four in the yard. The gussets out of the bosom, Pattern Plate II, Fig. 3 ; the back, Plate II, Fig. 4.

N. B. A breadth and two thirds of *Lancashire* Dowlas ⅞ wide, is equal in width to the size of the above shift, and cut out in the same manner. The third of the breadth which is taken off will make sleeves for any of the sizes.

SHIFT, N° 3. *How cut out.*

Seven yards and two nails make six shifts. The bodies three quarters and half quarter long, one whole breadth, and the fifth of a breadth for a gore in each, six yards and half a quarter make six bodies all but one gore ; the whole breadth crossed slanting down the middle, and the gore to the strait side. To determine the slope, measure the broad end of the gore (as directed below) at the opposite ends of the breadth, and cross it to each pin. One breadth doubled in five equal parts, and crossed (allowing the top of the gore, three quarters of a nail wide), makes five gores, the one wanting will be the fifth of a breadth, three quarters and half a quarter long. Three quarters and one nail and half nail doubled in four, and the width of the breadth doubled in seven, make fourteen sleeves, one quarter and an inch wide ; the width of three sleeves and a half in the breadth. The gussets out of the bosom, Pattern Plate IX, Fig. 1 ; back, Plate IX, Fig. 2.

N. B. A breadth and a half of *Lancashire* Dowlas ⅞ wide, is equal in width to the size of the above shift made of yard wide *Irish*, and cut out in the same manner as the shift, N° 2.

SHIFT, Nº 4, or fourth size.

		Yds.	Qrs.	Nails.
Six bodies	—	4	2	0
Sleeves	— —	0	2	1

				s.	d.
		5	0	1	Value 5 : 1

		s.	d.
Price of each	—	0	10
Deduct a 4ᵗʰ	—	0	2½
Sold at	—	0	8

STAYS. Made of Duck, 11 d. *per* yard, runs three quarters and half a nail wide, and cane split once, sold at 1 s. *per* pound, which is about one halfpenny *per* yard. Coloured laces round or flat, ell long, tagged at both ends, 2 s. 10 d. the grofs, which contains 12 dozen. Whited brown thread 2 s. 10 d. *per* pound.

STAYS, Nº 1, or largest size.

			s.	d.
Three quarters of a yard of duck	—		0	8¼
Lace, cane, and thread	—	—	0	1¾
Price	—		0	10
Deduct a 4ᵗʰ	—		0	2½
Sold at	—		0	7½

SHIFT, N° 4. *How cut out.*

Five yards and half a quarter make six shifts. The bodies three quarters long, the breadth doubled, and the gore taken off the whole side, and * divided, and put on the other, the strait sides together. Half a yard and a nail make six pair of sleeves, the length of three in the length, and the width of four in the width of the cloth. The guffets out of the bosom, Pattern Plate I, Fig. 3. The pattern of the back, Plate I, Fig. 4.

STAYS, N° 1. *How cut out.*

Three quarters, two nails and a half make one pair double, and one half of a back single. There will be a front and one half of a back in the width. When the above quantity is taken from the piece, double down one side to the width of the half front of the stays, Pattern Plate VIII, Fig. 3, and lay the front to the whole side where the cloth is doubled, then cut the half back out of the remainder of the width of the cloth, Pattern Plate X, Fig. 1. Do this a second time, and then double the remainder of the cloth, the width in three, which will make three half backs single, and a piece for the shoulder-straps, Pattern Plate X, Fig. 4, a quarter and a nail long, and three quarters of a nail wide, doubled. Cases must be backstitched down the stays of the width of the cane, four in the back, two in the front, two slanting as a stomacher, and one piece round the breast; for which, and also for the proper distances of the lace-holes, see the patterns of the smallest size; the lace-holes for the opposite side are marked by dots on the edge of the pattern, and the distances of those in the larger sized stays may be proportioned accordingly. Two yards a quarter and half of split cane.

---

* *N. B.* This is generally thought unnecessary work; but the shape of the shift is much better, than when the slant is joined to the strait side.

D

S T A Y S, N° 2, or second size.

		s.	d.
Half a yard, and one nail and a half of duck — — —		0 :	6¾
Cane, lace, and thread — —		0 :	1½
	Price —	0 :	8¼
	Deduct a 4th —	0 :	2
	Sold at —	0 :	6

S T A Y S, N° 3, or third size.

		s.	d.
Half a yard of duck — —		0 :	5½
Cane, lace, and thread — —		0 :	1½
	Price —	0 :	7
	Deduct a 4th —	0 :	1½
	Sold at —	0 :	5½

STAYS, N° 2. *How cut out.*

Half a yard, one nail and a half; make one pair double, and there will be a front and two half backs in the width. Double the breadth down the middle, and lay the front of Pattern Plate VIII, Fig. 4, to the whole fide, and the back part, Pattern Plate X, Fig. 2, to the felvedge. *N. B.* By laying the patterns on again with the bottoms oppofite to thofe already cut out, a flope will come out, which will make the two fhoulder ftraps a quarter long. Two yards, two nails and a half of fplit cane.

STAYS, N° 3. *How cut out.*

Three quarters of a yard will make one pair of ftays and a half. Divide the width of the cloth in three, and each part will make a fingle front, (Pattern Plate VIII, Fig. 5), and two half backs, (Pattern Plate X, Fig. 3,) thus: Double the two ends together, and lay the front of the pattern to the whole end where doubled, by which the fronts will be cut whole before, and the remainder makes the backs. The fhoulder ftraps cut from the flopings at the bottom about a quarter long each. Two yards of fplit cane.

STOCKINGS.

The proper worsted for knitting the stockings is of four-threads, at two-pence an ounce; but if bought by the dozen pounds, is sold at twenty-four shillings the dozen, which is only three halfpence an ounce (sixteen ounces allowed to the pound). When the stockings are knitted, they must be weighed, and the value calculated at two-pence an ounce, which allows for the necessary waste in working; then the fourth part deducted from the price of the weight. The best colour for the girls is a light blue, and for the boys a mottled colour, either black or brown.

Knitting needles are generally sold in sets, four needles in each, at a penny the set; but if a quantity is purchased at a time, they are sold by the weight at one shilling the pound. A pound weight of needles of a proper size for coarse worsted contains 96 needles, which make twenty-four sets; and the price is by that means reduced to one halfpenny *per* set.

SHOES,

Are better ordered according to the measure wanted, and one fourth part of the price deducted when delivered to the purchaser, as they are much stronger than those that are bought ready made.

WORK-BAGS given as Rewards.

Made of mulberry colour ftuff, half yard wide, at 7 d. *per* yard. Three quarters and a nail to each, the felvedge run together at the fides, and a broad hem at the top to draw with a ftring, a yard and a quarter of tape the fame colour; three yards for one penny.

		s.	d.
Three quarters and a nail of ftuff	—	0 :	5¼
Tape and thread — —	—	0 :	0½
Price	—	0 :	6

N. B. In the middle of one fide of each work-bag fix a ticket of white cloth, (herring-boned on with thread the fame colour as the work-bag), on which print (with marking inftruments) the girl's name at length. A fmall pair of fciffars in a fheath, (2 s. and 3 s. *per* dozen), and a thimble (at 3½ d. *per* dozen) may be added to the prefent, and given to each girl when fhe has finifhed the firft pair of ftockings of her own knitting.

TIPPETS. Made of *Irish* Cloth, called $\frac{7}{8}$ of a yard wide, at 12 *d. per* yard; and yard wide, at 15 *d. per* yard. Tape 4½ *d.* the piece, containing 19 yards.

TIPPET, N° 1, or largest size, *Irish* $\frac{7}{8}$ wide.

	s.	d.
One quarter of a yard, and half a nail of cloth — — —	0 :	3½
Tape and thread — —	0 :	0½
Price —	0 :	4
Deduct a 4th —	0 :	1
Sold at —	0 :	3

TIPPET, N° 2, or smallest size, yard wide *Irish*.

	s.	d.
Three nails and a half of cloth —	0 :	3½
Tape and thread — — —	0 :	0½
Price —	0 :	4
Deduct a 4th —	0 :	1
Sold at —	0 :	3

N. B. The difference in the widths and price of the cloth make these two sizes of tippets the same price.

TIPPET, Nº 1. *How cut out.*

Half a yard and a nail make two. Double the breadth in the middle, and then double down the end as deep as the width of the Pattern Plate XI, placing the back to the whole side of the breadth where doubled, which when cut out will make two at once. Three quarters and a half of tape, the neck sewed upon it, and some gathers on each side.

TIPPET, Nº 2. *How cut out.*

Three quarters and a half make four. The breadth doubled down the middle, and the Pattern Plate XII, laid across, cutting out one below the other. The neck sewed upon a tape (the same as Nº 1), three quarters and a half long, rather more gathers on each side than are necessary for the pattern of the largest size.

N. B. It is better to make them of any kind of cheap printed Linen or striped Holland.

D 4

The EXPENCE of CLOATHING
for a GIRL of the largeft Size, with One Fourth of the Value deducted.

	s.	d.
A Check Apron	1	7
A Black Stuff Bonnet	0	8½
A Cap	0	4½
A Grey Duffeild Cloak	3	0
A Stuff Gown	3	7½
A Check Neck Handkerchief	0	9
A Pair of Black Worfted Gloves	0	8
A Linfey Woolfey Petticoat	2	1½
A Flannel Petticoat	1	7½
A Shift	1	6
A Pair of Stockings about	0	9
A Pair of Shoes	2	3
A Pair of Stays	0	7½
	19	7

CLOATHING for BOYS;

With One Fourth of the Price
deducted.

DIRECTIONS

RELATING TO

The cutting out of SHIRTS.

As most cloths, though called of one width, run very differently, such widths may be purchased as are nearest to those herein mentioned, and if not exactly the same, the difference, whether more or less, must go to the width of the body of the shirt, as it will be less material there than in the piece allotted for the wristbands, &c. which cannot allow of any alteration in their widths. Again; in cutting out a number of small pieces, such as gussets, wristbands, &c. it is better to measure the whole length necessary for the number wanted of each sort, and divide it equally; as by measuring, and cutting off one by one, it will be found hardly possible not to gain or lose upon the whole quantity: the greatest exactness must be observed in the measuring, which will be made easy by consulting the scale in Plate IV.

When

When a fet of fhirts are cut out, it is better to double the wriftbands in the middle, and the fhoulder ftraps the fides to the middle, to diftinguifh them, left any miftake fhould arife in making up the fhirt from their being fo nearly of a length; alfo each part of the fhirt fhould be pinned together with the fleeves, and folded up in the body. Then fix a paper ticket about two or three inches fquare with pafte upon the fhirt, leaving a blank at the upper part of the ticket for the name of the girl who makes it, and put the number of the fize, the price it cofts, and that which it is to be fold for, at the bottom. The fhifts, &c. may be ticketed in the fame manner.

SHIRTS. *Drogheda* or *Lancashire* cloth called $\frac{7}{4}$ of a yard wide, but measures three quarters and an inch only, at 10¼ *d. per* yard.

SHIRT, N° 1.

	Yds.	Qrs.	Nails.
Six bodies —	11 :	3 :	0½
Six pair sleeves —	3 :	3 :	0
Collars, &c. —	1 :	2 :	1½

				s.	d.
	17 :	0 :	2	Value 15 :	5

	s.	d.
Price of each —	2 :	7
Thread and buttons	0 :	1
	2 :	8
Deduct a 4th —	0 :	8
Sold at —	2 :	0

N. B. The price of the above cloths when purchased wholesale is only 10½ *d. per* yard.

SHIRT, N° 1. *Drogheda* or *Lancashire* cloth. *How cut out.*

Seventeen yards and half a quarter make fix shirts. The length for each body is two yards all but half a nail. The whole breadth in the width. Eleven yards, three quarters and half a nail make fix bodies. The sleeves half a yard long, all but half a nail. Three yards and three quarters make the twelve sleeves, one sleeve and a half in the breadth, first taking off of the width of the breadth one nail, which in the length of the three yards and three quarters for the sleeves makes fix pair of shoulder straps, and two pair of wristbands a quarter long each, all but a quarter of a nail. The length of one sleeve makes a pair of either. Three quarters of a yard and a nail make fix collars, two in the length, a quarter and a half, and half a nail long; and the width of three in the width of the cloth, which makes them a full quarter wide. One quarter makes twelve sleeve gussets, half a quarter square, viz. the width of two on the selvedge side, and fix in the width of the cloth. One quarter all but a quarter of a nail, (the width of the cloth doubled in twelve), makes the four pair of wristbands which are wanting to complete the fix pair, and two pair over. One quarter and half a nail make twenty-four neck and side gussets, a nail and a half square; the width of three on the selvedge side, and eight in the width of the cloth.

N. B. In cutting out three sets, or one dozen and a half of shirts, as above, a quarter of a yard will be saved in the last half dozen; as the two pair of wristbands, over the number required in the two first sets, will supply the four pair wanting to complete the third set.

SHIRTS. *Drogbeda* or *Lancashire* cloth, at 10¾ *d.* per yard.

SHIRT, N° 2, or smallest size.

	Yds.	Qrs.	Nails.
Six bodies, &c. —	9	3	0
Six pair of sleeves —	2	2	2

			s.	d.
12 : 1 : 2	Value	11 : 1½

	s.	d.
Price of each —	1 :	10¾
Thread and buttons	0 :	1¾
	2 :	0
Deduct a 4th —	0 :	6
Sold at —	1 :	6

N. B. There are only two sizes of the Shirts made of the *Drogbeda* cloth, as it is only proper for the larger working boys.

SHIRT, N° 2. *Drogheda* or *Lancashire* cloth.
How cut out.

Twelve yards and a half and two nails make six shirts. The length for each body is a yard and a half, and half a quarter; half yard, half quarter, and nail wide. Nine yards and three quarters make six bodies. Before the lengths for the bodies are cut off, take one nail and a half off of the width of the cloth; which piece makes the collars, wristbands, shoulder-straps, sleeve guffets, neck and side guffets, and is cut out as follows: The width makes half a collar, one quarter and a half long. Four yards and a half make twelve half collars. It next makes the width of two wristbands or shoulder-straps: the wristbands (half the length of the collar) three nails long: and one yard and a half quarter make the six pair. The shoulder-straps three nails and a half long, and one yard, quarter and nail, make the six pair. Again; one sleeve guffet in the width, one nail and a half square, and one yard and half a quarter make the twelve guffets. The remainder of the piece (being one yard and three quarters all but one nail in length) doubled into twenty-four, makes the neck and side guffets, taking off so much of the width as will leave them square.

Two yards, two quarters, and half a quarter of the *Lancashire* cloth, make six pair of sleeves, viz. one pair in the width of the cloth, one quarter, one half quarter, and one nail long.

N. B. There are no sleeve pieces allowed for in shirts made of this cloth, it being so thick, the sleeve is better put in without.

SHIRTS, Nº 1. Yard wide *Irish*, at 12 *d.*

SHIRT, Nº 1, or largest size.

	Yds.	Qrs.	Nails.
Six bodies, &c. —	12	0	0
Six pair of sleeves, &c.	4	0	0

16 : 0 : 0 Value 16 : 0

	s.	d.
Price of each —	2	8
Thread and buttons	0	1
	2	9
Deduct a 4th —	0	8¼
Sold at —	2	1

SHIRT, Nº 1. Yard wide *Irish. How cut out.*

Sixteen yards make six shirts. The length for each body is two yards, and the width three quarters, one nail and a half. Twelve yards make six bodies. Before the lengths for the bodies are cut off, take half a quarter and half a nail off the width of the cloth, which piece furnishes all the parts belonging to the six shirts (except eight sleeve pieces, which are supplied from the sleeves) and is cut out as follows. The width makes half a collar, a quarter, half quarter, and half a nail long. Four yards, three quarters, and half a quarter make the twelve half collars. One sleeve gusset in the width, first

taking

taking off the felvedge, will be half a quarter, and near half a nail fquare. One yard and three quarters make the twelve guffets. The cloth is not wide enough for the width of two neck or fide guffets; but it will make the width of one, and a flip a nail wide, which will be the width of the piece for the infide of the fleeves. Two yards and a quarter in length therefore will make twenty-four fmall guffets a nail and a half fquare, and four fleeve pieces and a half, half a yard long. The width makes the width of two wriftbands or fhoulder-ftraps. The wriftbands one quarter long. One yard and a half will make the fix pair. The fhoulder-ftraps one quarter, and a quarter of a nail long. One yard and a half and two nails make the fix pair. This exactly ufes all the piece of cloth.

Four yards of the *Irifh* cloth make fix pair of fleeves, one and a half in the width of the cloth half a yard long, half a yard and half a quarter wide, firft taking off a flip a nail wide from the width of the cloth for the eight fleeve pieces wanting above, which doubled in eight makes them half a yard long, and with the four and a half cut out before completes twelve fleeve pieces and a half. This half overplus being a quarter of a yard in length, ferves to cut out hearts for the bofoms.

SHIRTS. Yard wide *Irish*, at 12 *d.*

SHIRT, N° 2.

		Yds.	Qrs.	Nails.		
Six bodies, &c.	–	10	: 2	: 0		
Six collars, &c.	–	0	: 3	: 1½		
					s.	*d.*
Call it 11½ yards		11	: 1	: 1½ Value	11	: 6

		s.	*d.*
Price of each	–	1	: 11
Thread and buttons		0	: 1
		2	: 0
Deduct a 4th	–	0	: 6
Sold at	–	1	: 6

SHIRT, N° 2. Yard wide *Irish. How cut out.*

Eleven yards and a half, and one nail and half make six shirts. The length for each body is one yard and three quarters; the width half a yard, half a quarter, and half a nail. Ten yards and a half make six bodies. Before the lengths for the bodies are cut off, take a quarter of a yard, and three quarters of a nail off of the width of the cloth, which piece makes the sleeves, wristbands, shoulder-straps, and sleeve pieces, cut out as follows. Half the sleeve (a quarter wide) and the width of one shoulder-strap, or wristband (three quarters of a nail wide) in the width. The sleeves one quarter, half quarter, and a nail long; so that the ten yards

3   and

and a half in length doubled into twenty-four, when the flip of three quarters of a nail wide is taken off, makes the fix pair of fleeves. The wriftbands half a quarter and one nail long: two yards and a quarter of the flip off the fleeve make the fix pair. Two yards and a half, and half a quarter make twelve fhoulder-ftraps, half a quarter, and one nail and a half long. The remainder doubled in twelve is exactly enough for the twelve fleeve pieces: one quarter and a half, and one nail and a half long each.

Three quarters, and one nail and a half of *Irifh* cloth make the collars, fleeve, neck, and fide guffets; viz. collars a quarter and a half long, the length of two in three quarters of a yard, and the width of three off of the width of the cloth, three nails wide each. This leaves one quarter and a half in the width of the breadth; and one nail and a half at the end of the collars, the latter doubled in twelve, makes the twelve fide guffets, which will allow of being cut fquare if they do not exactly run fo: the piece left will make twelve fleeve guffets, and twelve neck guffets; viz. the fleeve guffets half a quarter fquare, the width of three in the width of the cloth, and four on the felvedge fide in the length of half a yard. And the remaining piece (being one quarter in length, and one quarter and a half in breadth) makes the twelve neck guffets; viz. the width of three in the felvedge fide, and four in the width.

SHIRTS. Yard wide *Irish*, at 12 *d. per* yard.

SHIRT, N° 3.

	Yds.	Qrs.	Nails.		s.	d.
Six bodies, &c. &c. –	8 :	2 :	o	Value	8 :	6

		s.	d.
Price of each	–	1 :	5
Thread and buttons		o :	1
		1 :	6
Deduct a 4th	–	o :	4$\frac{1}{2}$
Sold at	–	1 :	1$\frac{1}{2}$

N. B. The Cloth is calculated only at eight yards and a half (though the bodies require nine yards in length to be cut off) becaufe there is an overplus of the piece that comes off of the bodies, after the fleeves and other pieces are cut out.

SHIRT, N° 3. Yard wide *Irish*. *How cut out.*

Nine yards make the length for fix bodies, one yard and a half each, half a yard and half a quarter wide all but about half a nail. Before the lengths for the bodies are cut off, take a quarter and half a quarter off of the width of the cloth, which piece is fufficient for the fleeves, and all the other parts of the fix fhirts; cut out as follows: The whole fleeve in the width (a quarter and half a quarter wide), a quarter and half a quarter long. Four
yards

yards and a half make the six pair. Two collars in the width, half a quarter and a nail wide each, and one quarter and a nail and a half long. A yard and half a nail will make six; viz. the width of two in the width, and the length of three in the length. The sleeve-guffets half a quarter square, half a yard makes twelve; viz. the width of three in the width, and four on the felvedge side. Half a yard more makes twenty-four neck and side guffets a nail and full half a nail square, and three wriftbands three quarters of a nail wide, half a quarter and half a nail long, thus; firft take off three nails from the width, and divide it in three for the wriftbands: the width of four guffets in the width of the remainder, and six in the length. A quarter, a nail and a half make eight pair of wriftbands; the length of two in the length, and the width of eight in the width. A quarter and a half make eight pair of shoulder-ftraps, a quarter and a nail long, the length of two in the length, and the width of eight in the width. The two pair of shoulder-ftraps, and the three pair and a half of wriftbands above the number wanted, will do for other shirts of the fame fize. Sleeve pieces one quarter, a half quarter and one nail long, and one nail wide; three quarters and half a quarter make twelve; viz. the length of two in the length, and the width of six in the width.

There will ftill remain three quarters and half a quarter in length overplus of the piece of cloth, which will help to make the collars, neck and side guffets, for the fets of shirts N° 2; and therefore fix shirts of the above fize are calculated only to contain eight yards and a half of cloth.

SUITS of CLOATHS.

Boys cloathing being very expensive on account of the making, it has been found impossible to reduce the prices in proportion to other articles. But as a general idea may be useful, a few examples of the modes of purchasing are added, with the prices affixed according to the different sizes, although bought on an average of one size with another at the same price. Which is done by taking the whole sum that three suits cost, and dividing it into three sums, each a proportion larger than the other. For instance, suits of cloaths of a coarse brown cloth have been made up in the country of three sizes at the average of 11 s. 3 d. the suit, fitting boys of six, ten, and fourteen years of age. Three times 11 s. 3 d. is 1 l. 13 s. 9 d. Charge the largest suit at 13 s. 3 d. the second size at 11 s. 3 d. and the smallest at 9 s. 3 d. which three sums will make exactly 1 l. 13 s. 9 d. The prices of the three sizes with the deduction of one fourth therefore will stand as follow.

SUIT, N° 1, or largest size.

		s.	d.
Price	—	13	: 3
Deduct a 4th	—	3	: 3
Sold at	—	10	: 0

SUIT, N° 2, or second size.

		s.	d.
Price	—	11	: 3
Deduct a 4th	—	2	: 9
Sold at	—	8	: 6

SUIT, N° 3, or smallest size.

		s.	d.
Price	—	9	: 3
Deduct a 4th	—	2	: 3
Sold at	—	7	: 0

SUITS of CLOATHS.

As it is feldom found that a poor labouring man can afford to purchafe a whole fuit of cloaths at once, even at the reduced prices, and as children may not be in want of a whole fuit at the fame time, for their convenience another divifion has been made of the whole reduced price into the three different articles, of coat, waiftcoat, and breeches. For inftance, the price of the largeft fized fuit with the fourth deducted, appears to be 10 s. (fee the preceding page), and if defired to be bought feparate, they are fold thus: the coat 5 s. the waiftcoat 2 s. and the breeches 3 s. which fums together make exactly 10 s. And the fmaller fuit in the fame manner, as fpecified in the following examples.

			s.	d.
COATS,	First fize –	Sold at	5 :	0
	Second fize –		4 :	6
	Third fize –		4 :	0

			s.	d.
WAISTCOATS,	First fize	Sold at	2 :	0
	Second fize		1 :	6
	Third fize		1 :	0

			s.	d.
BREECHES,	First fize –	Sold at	3 :	0
	Second fize		2 :	6
	Third fize –		2 :	0

Leather breeches for a boy of 12 years old coft 3 s. 6 d. fold at 2 s. 7½ d. and other prices according to the fize.

SUITS of CLOATHS.

Another way of providing the above commodity, and apparently the moft eligible, is by purchafing at the Slop Shops in *London*, where they are ready made, (or prepared immediately), of a much better and more durable quality than thofe before mentioned, with only a fmall addition to the price. For inftance, coats made of very ftrong cloths of various colours may be had at 7 s. 6 d. apiece, and three fmaller fizes at 5 s. 9 d. alfo red napped waiftcoats at 3 s. and three leffer fizes at 2 s. 3 d. each, of four different degrees of fize, fo as to allow the fmaller ones to be forted into two fizes. The beft method therefore is to buy one coat at 7 s. 6 d. and three at 5 s. 9 d. which will coft 1 l. 4 s. 9 d. and then calculate them in three fizes, viz. one at 7 s. 9 d. one at 6 s. 6 d. and two at 5 s. 3 d. which fums will amount exactly to 1 l. 4 s. 9 d. And the waiftcoats, four of which coft 9 s. 9 d. the fame, viz. calculate one at 3 s. 3 d. one at 2 s. 6 d. and two at 2 s. each, which amounts to 9 s. 9 d. With the fourth deducted, the price will be as follows.

COATS.

	Price	s.	d.	Sold at	s.	d.
Firft fize —		7	9		5	$9\frac{3}{4}$
Second fize		6	6		4	$10\frac{1}{2}$
Third fize		5	3		3	$11\frac{1}{4}$

WAISTCOATS.

	Price	s.	d.	Sold at	s.	d.
Firft fize —		3	3		2	$5\frac{1}{4}$
Second fize		2	6		1	$10\frac{1}{2}$
Third fize		2	0		1	6

WHITE KERSEY JACKETS.

Three fizes are made up in the country, at the average of 5 s. apiece, fitting boys of fix, ten, and fourteen years of age. The proportions, when fold feparate, are as follow.

JACKET, N° 1, or largeft fize.

		s.	d.
Price	—	5 :	6
Deduct a 4th	—	1 :	4½
Sold at	—	4 :	1½

JACKET, N° 2, or fecond fize.

		s.	d.
Price	—	5 :	0
Deduct a 4th	—	1 :	3
Sold at	—	3 :	9

JACKET, N° 3, or fmalleft fize.

		s.	d.
Price	—	4 :	6
Deduct a 4th	—	1 :	1½
Sold at	—	3 :	4½

WHITE NAPPED JACKETS.

Are ready made at the Slop fhops of five fizes, from N° 3, to N° 7. The larger at 2 *s.* 6 *d.* the fmaller at 2 *s.* apiece, one with another. To divide them into three, the fhop numbers (of which the greateft is the largeft fize) muft be charged as follow.

JACKET, N° 1, or largeft fize.

		s.	*d.*
Shop mark 7,	Price —	2 :	8
	Deduct a 4th —	0 :	8
	Sold at —	2 :	0

JACKET, N° 2, or fecond fize.

		s.	*d.*
Shop mark 6	Price of each	2 :	1
Ditto 5			
	Deduct a 4th	0 :	6¼
	Sold at —	1 :	7

JACKET, N° 3, or fmalleft fize.

		s.	*d.*
Shop mark 4	Price of each	1 :	6
Ditto 3			
	Deduct a 4th	0 :	4½
	Sold at —	1 :	1½

DRAB BREECHES.

Are ready made at the Slop fhops of five fizes from Nº 3, to Nº 7. The largeft at 2 s. the fmaller at 1 s. 6 d. a pair, one with another. To divide them into three fizes, the fhop numbers (of which the greateft is the largeft fize) muft be charged as follow.

DRAB BREECHES, Nº 1, or largeft fize.

			s.	d.
Shop mark	7	Price of each	1 :	9
Ditto	6	Deduct a 4th	0 :	5¼
		Sold at —	1 :	4

DRAB BREECHES, Nº 2, or fecond fize.

			s.	d.
Shop mark	5	Price of each	1 :	6
Ditto	4	Deduct a 4th	0 :	4½
		Sold at —	1 :	1½

DRAB BREECHES, Nº 3, or fmalleft fize.

		s.	d.
Shop mark 3,	Price —	1 :	3
	Deduct a 4th — 0 -		3¾
	Sold at —	0 :	11

HATS.

HAT, Nº 1, or largeſt ſize.

		s.	d.
Price	—	2 :	6
Deduct a 4th	—	0 :	$7\frac{1}{2}$
Sold at	—	1 :	$10\frac{1}{2}$

HAT, Nº 2, or ſecond ſize.

		s.	d.
Price	—	2 :	0
Deduct a 4th	—	0 :	6
Sold at	—	1 :	6

HAT, Nº 3, ſmalleſt ſize.

		s.	d.
Price	—	1 :	6
Deduct a 4th	—	0 :	$4\frac{1}{2}$
Sold at	—	1 :	$1\frac{1}{2}$

N. B. The above article is calculated at the retail prices. The wholeſale prices of Nº 2, and Nº 3, are 1 s. 9 d. and 1 s. 5 d.

CLOATHING
For POOR WOMEN.

OBSERVATIONS.

As this fubject and the two following, namely, the Cloathing for poor Men, and the inftructions for providing fets of Childbed Linen for the ufe of poor married Women, are matters of private charity, only, the calculation of their value is ftated at the full price of the materials wholefale, but without any addition for the expence of making up the different articles, as thofe who undertake to prepare them by the directions herein laid down, will moft probably have them compleated in their own houfes; but if the further benefit is wifhed, of employing fome poor Woman to make them up, the additional price of the labour is eafily added to the value of each article. It may not be improper to obferve in this place, that the kindeft and moft real charity to the poor, is to adopt fuch modes of relief to their neceffities as will at the fame time promote their induftry: the fruit of their own labour will always be more ferviceable to them, and perhaps it may be in the experience of many, that it is frequently more acceptable to them, and more gratefully acknowledged than actual Donations alone.

BONNETS,

Made of black Durant, called yard wide, but
measures three quarters and half a nail only,
at 15 *d. per* yard. Pasteboard 2 *d. per* sheet.
Strings of black Quality shoe binding 2 *s.* the
piece, containing 32 yards.

How cut out.

One yard and a quarter make one bonnet with
a binder, and half a front. A sheet of pasteboard
makes one front, Pattern Pl. I, Fig. 5, and one
front of the largest size of the girls bonnets in the
width. Half a yard and half a quarter of stuff
makes a caul and half the front, in the width, thus;
place the pattern lengthways with the edge to
the selvedge, and when cut out, the remainder of
the breadth will make the caul, allowing for a
broad hem, the selvedge at the bottom. Half a
yard and half a quarter more, will make two half
fronts (cut one out of the other); and a piece that
will serve for a binder hemmed at the sides. One
yard of binding for the strings.

	s.	d.
Stuff — — —	1	4
Pasteboard, strings, and thread —	0	2
The price of one bonnet —	1	6

C A P S,

Made of *Irish* cloth called yard wide, at 15 *d. per* yard, but meafures three quarters and three nails and a half only. Trimmed with *Hanover* lace, at 1 *s.* 9 *d.* the piece, containing 9 yards, which is about 2½ *d. per* yard. *Holland* tape 3½ *d.* the piece, containing 18 yards and a half.

How cut out.

Half a yard, three nails and a quarter make four caps, which may be cut out all together, thus; when this quantity of cloth is cut off, double the width in four, and then double the length in half, laying the Pattern Pl. IX, Fig. 3, upon it with the front to the fide of the cloth where the felvedge is, and the top of the headpiece to that end which is whole, where the cloth is doubled. When it is opened, the four caps are to be divided from one another, and a fmall flope cut to the forehead on the top of the headpieces, where they join. A broad hem at the bottom of the caul behind. One yard and half a quarter of *Hanover* lace for the border. One yard of narrow tape for the ftrings.

	s.	d.
About four nails of *Irish* — —	0 :	2¼
One yard, and two nails of *Hanover* lace —	0 :	3
Tape and thread — — —	0 :	0¼
The price of one cap —	**0 :**	**5½**

C L O A K S.

Made of grey Duffeild or Coating, at 2 s. *per* yard, called yard wide, but meafures three quarters and half a quarter only. Narrow worfted ferret for the binding, at 11 *d.* the piece, containing 30 yards. Ditto broader for the ftrings, at 20 *d.* the piece, containing 32 yards and three quarters. Grey thread 3 s. *per* pound.

How cut out.

Two yards and a half of Duffeild make a cloak; viz. two yards in the width of the cloak, the whole width in the length. A flope in the neck a nail deep flanting about half way on each fide of the neck. A fmall flope at the bottom of the cloak to form the elbow. Pieces like gores near a quarter wide, taken off in the front of the cloak from the top, floping to a point about half way down the forepart, the broad ends turned to the bottom, and the pieces joined like gores to the remaining ftrait part of the front to form the flope. The hood a quarter and half deep; the width of the cloth round the face; the corners floped off at the back of the head, half a quarter from the crown, and a fmall flope in the neck. The remaining half quarter of the duffeild makes the collar.

Two yards and three quarters of narrow binding for the front of the cloak. A yard and a quarter of the broad binding for the neck, and three quarters of a yard of ditto, for two ftrings to tie acrofs the breaft.

		s.	d.
Two yards and a half of duffeild	—	5 :	0
Binding and thread — —	—	0 :	6
The price of one cloak	—	5 :	6

GOWNS.

Made of Grogram at 12 *d. per* yard, called yard wide, but meafures three quarters and a half quarter only. The body-lining of brown *Holland*, at 9 *d. per* yard, called $\frac{7}{8}$ wide, but meafures three quarters and half a nail only. Coloured thread, 3 *s. per* pound.

	s.	d.
Six yards of Grogram — —	6	0
One yard of brown *Holland* —	0	9
Thread — — —	0	1
The price of one gown —	6	10

PETTICOATS.

Made of ftriped Linfey woolfey, at 11 *d. per* yard, called yard wide, but meafures three quarters and a half only. Bound with tape at 11 *d.* the piece, containing 29 yards.

	s.	d.
Three yards, (the felvedge round) —	2	9
One yard and a half of tape, and thread —	0	1
The price of one petticoat —	2	10

PETTICOATS.

Made of Flannel, at 12 *d. per* yard, called yard wide, but meafures three quarters one nail and a half only. Bound with tape, at 11 *d.* the piece, containing 29 yards.

	s.	d.
Two yards and a half, (the felvedge round)	2	6
One yard and a half of tape, and thread	0	1
The price of one flannel petticoat —	2	7

S H I F T S.

Made of Dowlas, at 12 *d. per* yard, called ⅞ wide, but meafures three quarters of a yard and three quarters of a nail only. And yard wide *Irifh* Cloth, at 12 *d. per* yard, for the fleeves.

How cut out.

Two ells in one fhift, the whole width of the cloth; the gore taken from one fide, and put on the other. One yard and a quarter of *Irifh* make four pair of fleeves, one pair in the width, (firft taking off three nails for the wriftbands), and the length of four fleeves in the ell. Pattern of the back, Pl. II, Fig. 5; and of the bofom, Pl. II, Fig. 6. The guffets out of the bofom.

	s.	d.
Two yards and a half of Dowlas —	2 :	6
One quarter and a nail of *Irifh* — —	0 :	3¾
Thread — — — —	0 :	0¼
The price of one fhift —	2 :	10

A P R O N S.

Made of Check at 1 *s.* 10 *d. per* yard, called yard and half wide, but meafures one yard one quarter and a nail only. Tape for the binding at 6¾ *d.* the piece, containing 19 yards.

	s.	d.
One yard and a nail of check —	1 :	11½
Two yards of tape and thread —	0 :	1
The price of one apron —	2 :	0½

The EXPENCE of CLOATHING
for a Poor WOMAN.

	l.	*s.*	*d.*
A Gown of Grogram —	0 :	6 :	10
A Linsey Woolsey Petticoat —	0 :	2 :	10
A Flannel ditto — —	0 :	2 :	7
A Dowlas Shift — —	0 :	2 :	10
A Check Apron — —	0 :	2 :	0½
A Cap with a Border — —	0 :	0 :	5½
A Double Check Handkerchief	0 :	0 :	10
A Pair of Black Worsted Stockings	0 :	1 :	2
A Pair of Black Worsted Mitts	0 :	0 :	10
A Black Stuff Bonnet —	0 :	1 :	6
A Pair of Shoes, ready made —	0 :	2 :	9
A Grey Duffeild Cloak —	0 :	5 :	6
	1 :	10 :	2

CLOATHING
For POOR MEN.

S H I R T S.

Made of Dowlas at 11 *d. per* yard, called $\frac{7}{8}$ wide, but meafures three quarters of a yard and three quarters of a nail only. Buttons at 7 *d. per* grofs.

	l.	s.	d.
Twenty-one yards and a half of Dowlas	0	19	$8\frac{1}{2}$
Buttons and thread — —	0	0	$3\frac{1}{2}$
	1	0	0
The price of one fhirt —	0	3	4

SHIRTS of Dowlas. *How cut out.*

Twenty-one yards and a half make fix fhirts; the bodies two yards and a quarter in length each. Thirteen yards and a half make fix bodies. The fleeves half a yard and half a quarter long; one fleeve and a half in the width of the cloth; five yards make the fix pair. The collars half a yard long, a quarter of a yard and a quarter of a nail wide; one yard makes fix, the width of three in the width, and the length of two in the length. One quarter and a nail make the twenty-four neck and fide guffets, a nail and a half fquare; viz. the width of eight in the width of the cloth, and three on the felvedge fide. Half a yard and three quarters of a nail (the felvedge cut off) make the twelve fleeve guffets, (half a quarter of a yard and above three quarters of a nail fquare); viz. the width of three guffets on the felvedge fide, and four in the width of the cloth. Half a yard and a quarter of a nail make the twelve wriftbands, and twelve fhoulder-ftraps; viz. twelve in the width of the cloth; the length of a wriftband (a quarter long) and a fhoulder-ftrap (a quarter of a yard and a quarter of a nail long) on the felvedge fide. Half a yard and half a quarter, the width of the cloth doubled in twelve, make the twelve fleeve pieces, half a yard and half a quarter long.

The EXPENCE of CLOATHING
for a Poor M A N.

	l.	s.	d.
A Suit of Cloaths of Brown Cloth —	0	19	0
A Dowlas Shirt — — —	0	3	4
* A Pair of Shoes — —	0	6	6
A Pair of knit Stockings —	0	1	6
A Hat — — —	0	2	4
	1	12	8

* Shoes may be had ready made at 5 s. the pair, but they are of a very inferior quality.

CHILD-BED LINEN

For the Use of the POOR.

BEDGOWNS.

Made of * printed linen, at 15 *d. per* yard, called three quarters wide, but meafures two quarters and three nails only. Tape 6¾ *d.* the piece, containing 19 yards.

	s.	d.
Two yards and a quarter of linen —	2 :	9¼
Tape — — —	0 :	0¼
	2 :	10

The price of one bedgown is 1 *s.* 5 *d.* without trimming.

BEDGOWNS. *How cut out.*

Two yards and a quarter make two bedgowns. Half a quarter, a nail and half, make four fleeves; the length of the four in the width of the linen, half a quarter and near a nail long. A full nail

* *N. B.* It will be better to chufe a pattern that does not go any particular way; for the gores being cut one out of the other, in cutting out four, the pattern muft in two of them run upwards, and in the other two downwards; which looks awkward when joined to the bedgown if a different way. But even in this cafe when two bedgowns are to be made of linen of the fame pattern, the gores, fleeves, and cuffs, when cut out as directed, may always be forted to have the pattern run the fame way as that on the bedgown to which they belong, provided care is taken that the bedgowns themfelves are made with the patterns contrary in each, which depends on the end that is fixed upon to cut for the neck.

cut

cut off from the length of each, and fewed on again, the wrong fide to the right fide of the fleeve, to turn up for the cuff. One quarter, half a quarter, and a full nail, make four gores, the width of the linen doubled in four and croffed to a point, the whole ones divided, to join to the ftrait fide of the bedgown. The remaining piece of linen divided for the two bedgowns, three quarters and half a nail long each. The bedgown doubled down the middle, and the back, Pattern Pl. VII, Fig. 3, and the bofom, Pattern Pl. VII, Fig. 4, cut out. The back being narrower than the bofom, allows the bedgown to fold over before. Then the fides of the breadth doubled to the middle, and creafed down the fides by a thread as near as poffible, and opened the length of the gore. The width of the fleeve meafured from the top of the bedgown, (where the fleeve is to be put in), and the bedgown cut about half a nail deep under the fleeve; the piece floped off to meet the gores.

N. B. Thefe bedgowns fit better in the waift, if inftead of the above, there is a piece a nail deep cut out under the arm, and ftrait down the body half a quarter long, which will form a plait at the hips; four ftrings may be placed oppofite to each other in the back, about a nail afunder, to tie the bedgown in if needful. The neck will allow of a hem, to draw with narrow tape. Four ftrings to tie before. If the bedgown is not cut to fold over before, it will alfo require four fmall plaits in the back: in that cafe, the back of the neck muft be allowed the fame width as the bofom, and a ftring put in to draw round, before the plaits in the back are made. A little *Hanover* lace to trim the neck makes them look neat.

SHIRTS, CAPS, and UNDER CAPS.

Made of Long Lawn, called yard wide, but meafures three quarters and a full nail only, at
2 s. 6 d. per yard. *Hanover* lace, at 10 d. the
piece, containing nine yards, which is near 1¾ d.
per yard.

	s.	d.
Two yards and a quarter of long lawn —	5 :	7½
Three yards of *Hanover* lace —	0 :	3½
	5 :	11
The price of one fhirt is about —	0 :	11¾

C A P S.

	s.	d.
Three quarters of long lawn —	1 :	10½
Five yards and a half of *Hanover* lace —	0 :	6
	2 :	4½
The price of one cap —	0 :	4¼

SHIRTS. *How cut out.*

Two yards and a quarter make fix fhirts. The body half a yard and half a quarter wide, and a quarter and a half long, the remainder of the width of the cloth makes the fleeves, one pair in the length of the fhirt, three nails fquare. The fhirt doubled down the middle, and the back Pl. VII, Fig. 9, and the bofom, Pl. VII, Fig. 10, cut out. The width of the back being lefs than the bofom, allows the fhirt to fold over before about half a nail, which makes it a much better fhape. The opening for the fleeves, a full nail and a half long. The guffets out of the bofom. The neck trimmed with half a yard of *Hanover* lace.

CAPS. *How cut out.*

Three quarters of a yard make fix caps; viz. the width divided in three. The width of the thirds will be the depth of the cap with double headpiece; two caps in the length of each third; cut out as follows: double down fuch a width for the headpiece as the depth of the Pattern Pl. IV, Fig. 2, will allow; then double the length of the cloth in four, (which will be the fize of the pattern), and cut out two caps at once, taking care that it is doubled exactly even, and pinning the pattern fteady, on account of the points of the caul. The headpiece is backftitched down. The cap joined behind; the two corners backftitched upon the hind part of the cap, and the middle point upon them, which forms the caul, and makes it ferve either for boys or girls. A hem for a ftring to draw behind. Three quarters and a half of *Hanover* lace.

N. B. One piece of *Hanover* lace trims fix caps, and fix fhirts, and there will be one yard and a nail over.

UNDER CAPS. *How cut out.*

Half a yard and half a quarter of long lawn make fix under caps. One quarter three nails and a half off of the width, make fix double headpieces, the whole width of three in the width, and the length of two in the length. Divide the width in three, then double each piece down the middle, and twice in the length, which will make it the fize of the half headpiece, Pattern Pl. VI, Fig. 2. Laying the top of the headpiece to the whole end, and cutting out two at once. For the cauls, double the remaining piece of long lawn, (which will be a quarter, a nail and a half wide), down the middle, lay the pattern of the whole caul, Pl. VI, Fig. 3, open upon it flanting with the narrow part as near oppofite to the corner as the width of the piece of the cloth will allow to take the pattern in; this will cut them bias; three in the length (and fomething over), which being double completes the fix cauls. When they are made up, the bottom of the caul is narrow hemmed, and the top put in with fmall plaits to fit the headpiece.

	s.	d.
Half a yard and half a quarter of long lawn	1 :	$6\frac{3}{4}$

The price of one under cap —	0 :	3

F R O C K S.

Made of printed Cotton, at 2 *s.* a yard, called yard wide, but measures three quarters and near a nail only. Body-lining of *Irish* cloth, called yard wide, and measures a yard all but half a nail, at 15 *d. per* yard. Tape 6¾ *d.* the piece, containing 19 yards.

How cut out.

Three yards make two frocks. A quarter and half and a nail, make the whole of the two bodies as follows: take off one quarter and half a nail for the bodies, cuffs, and shoulder-straps, measure half a yard and half a nail of the width of the cotton, and double that quantity down the middle the selvedge way; place the Pattern Pl. VII, Fig. 5, the fore-part of the body to the whole part of the cotton as doubled; when that is cut out, lay it on again below for the second body. The piece left of the width of the cotton is for the cuffs and shoulder straps, double it in half the selvedge at the end, and lay the Pattern Pl. VII, Fig. 6, lengthways for the cuffs, it will be the width for two, cut one out of the other, which (the cotton being doubled) will make four. The piece still remaining in the width will make the four shoulder-straps, Pl. VII, Fig. 7, the width of two in the width, and the length of two in the length. As there is a variation in the width of cottons, though called the same, the shoulder-straps will be sometimes wide enough to use double, and sometimes will require a lining. The remainder of the piece which was cut off for the bodies, &c. being half a quarter and half a nail, the width doubled in four makes the four sleeves, Pattern Pl. VII, Fig. 8. The remainder of the three yards of cotton, (which is two yards and a half, and one nail)

nail) divided into four breadths makes the two
fkirts, two breadths in each, without any flope.
The body and fkirt together will be three quarters
and a half long. A piece of narrow tape put
within the bottom of the body where the fkirt is
fewed in, ftrengthens it and prevents the waift
from ftretching. A ftring to draw round the
neck, and three on each fide to tie behind.
Half a quarter of yard wide *Irifh* doubled the
breadth in three, makes one body-lining and a
half, with a good allowance to turn in at the
back, or to fupply the lining for the fhoulder-
ftraps when wanted.

> *N. B.* Attention muft be paid in cutting out
> things that have a right and a wrong fide,
> that the fleeves and cuffs are not all cut for
> the fame arm. This may be done by taking
> care when two things are cut out at once,
> that the fame fides of the cotton, whether
> right fide or wrong, always face each other.
> In cutting out two frocks doubled as above
> directed, they will be right, only obferving
> in printed cottons that the patterns are laid
> on, fo that the flowers or ftripes may all go
> the fame way in the bodies, fkirts, &c.

				s.	d.
Three yards of cotton	—		—	6	0
Body-linings	—	—	—	0	5
Tape and thread	—		—	0	1
				6	6
The price of one frock			—	3	3

ROBE BLANKET.

Made of Linfey Flannel, at 1 s. 3 d. *per* yard, called yard wide, but meafures three quarters and three nails only. Statute Galloon for binding 4 s. the piece, containing 36 yards and a half, which is rather more than three farthings *per* yard.

How cut out.

Three quarters of a yard and a nail of flannel make one blanket; doubled in half down the middle. Gores cut from the felvedge fides, a quarter and half a nail wide at the top, and half a quarter, and half a nail wide at the bottom. The floped fides of the gores joined to the blanket. A ftrait piece cut out of the back (as it is doubled) a nail deep, and two nails and a quarter long, which will form a plait in the back of the fkirt, alfo the flope in the body cut ftrait, two nails and a quarter under the armhole, which will form fmall plaits at the hips, and make the waift fit better, the armhole cut out, and the corners rounded in front, Pattern Pl. XIII, Fig. 1, (which allows for the joining under the arm in the width of the armhole). The blanket to be bound all round with three yards and a half of Galloon, run on the edge of the infide, and turned back and fewed down upon the outfide of the blanket.

	s.	d.
Three quarters and a nail of flannel —	1	0¼
Three yards and a half of binding, and thread — — —	0	5¾
The price of one robe blanket —	1	6

SQUARES of DIAPER.

Made of figured Diaper, called ell wide, but measures a yard, one nail and a quarter only. Ten shillings the piece, which contains seven yards and a quarter. Two pieces divided each into twelve, make 24 squares of diaper double, half a yard and near a nail wide, but not quite square.

	l.	s.	d.
Two dozen squares of diaper double –	1	0	0

SQUARES of FLANNEL.

One yard and three quarters of white baize flannel, called yard wide, but measures three quarters and a half only, at 11½ d. *per* yard, which make two squares.

	s.	d.
* One yard and three quarters of white baize	1	8¾

* *N. B.* This being very necessary and useful to the poor women, it is not required to be returned with the Childbed linen.

SHIFTS.

Made of *Irish* cloth, at 14 *d. per* yard, called yard wide, and which measures a yard all but half a nail. *Hanover* lace, at 1 *s.* 4½ *d.* the piece, containing 9 yards.

How cut out.

Three yards three quarters and one nail make two shifts. The bodies one yard, one quarter, and one half quarter in the length of each. The whole breadth doubled like a shirt, sloped at the sides; the slope a nail wide at the shoulder, and cut to a point at the bottom. The back, Pattern Pl. III, Fig. 3, and the bosom, Pattern Pl. III, Fig. 4, to be cut out without dividing them from each other, as it will allow the gussets (which are cut from this piece) to be larger. One yard and a nail make the four sleeves, two in the width of the cloth, half a yard and half a nail long. The wristbands (made out of the sloping that comes off of the sides of the shift), a quarter long, to button with one button. The bosom opened a quarter deep, and a hem to draw with narrow tape before, as far as the turning on each side. One ell of *Hanover* lace, to trim the neck.

	s.	d.
Three yards, three quarters and a nail of *Irish*	4	5½
Two yards and a half of *Hanover* lace	0	4½
Tape, thread, and buttons	0	1
	4	11
The price of one shift	2	5½

S K I R T S.

Made of figured diaper, $7\frac{1}{2}$ d. *per* yard, half yard wide. Twelve yards make two skirts, five breadths in each skirt, and a yard doubled down the middle for the band; the skirt plaited into the band, the most plaits before.

	s.	d.
Twelve yards of diaper - -	7	6
The price of one skirt -	3	9

S H E E T S.

Made of *Lancashire* sheeting, at 14 d. *per* yard, called $\frac{9}{8}$ wide, but measures a full yard only, 52 yards in the piece, which make four pair. Three yards and a quarter all but half a nail long, two breadths in the sheet. Twelve yards, three quarters and a half quarter make one pair.

	s.	d.
The price of one pair of sheets -	15	1

P I L L O W C A S E S.

Made of *Irish* called $\frac{7}{8}$ wide, 12 d. a yard. Two yards make a pair, the selvedges at the ends.

	s.	d.
The price of one pillow case -	1	0

The EXPENCE of a Set of CHILD-BED LINEN to lend to the POOR.

		l.	s.	d.
2	Frocks — — —	0	6	6
2	Bedgowns — —	0	2	10
6	Shirts — —	0	5	11
6	Caps — — —	0	2	$4\frac{1}{2}$
6	Under caps — — —	0	1	$6\frac{3}{4}$
24	Squares of double Diaper —	1	0	0
2	Robe blankets — —	0	3	0
$1\frac{3}{4}$	Yards of white Baize flannel —	0	1	$8\frac{3}{4}$
2	Shifts — —	0	4	11
2	Skirts — — —	0	7	6
1	Pair of sheets — —	0	15	1
2	Pillow-cases — —	0	2	0
		3	13	5

A LIST of the various Articles and Materials neceſſary to be purchaſed for making up CLOATHING for the POOR, and the Wholeſale Prices of each.

	l.	s.	d.	
Stuff half a yard wide — — — —	0	16	3	the piece 29¼ yards.
Black Durant — — — —	0	1	1	*per* yard.
Linſey Woolſey — — — —	0	0	11	Dᵒ
Grogram — — — —	0	0	12	Dᵒ
Iriſh yard wide — — — —	0	1	0	Dᵒ
Ditto ⅞ — — — —	0	1	0	Dᵒ
Scotch cloth three quarters wide — —	0	0	9	Dᵒ
Lancaſhire Dᵒ ⅞ — — —	0	0	10½	Dᵒ
Duck Dᵒ Dᵒ — — —	0	0	11	Dᵒ
Check three quarters wide — — —	0	1	0	Dᵒ
Ditto yard and half wide — — —	0	1	10	Dᵒ
Worſted — — — —	1	4	0	1 dozen pound.
Paſteboard — — — —	0	0	2	*per* ſheet.
Statute Galloon — — —	0	4	0	the piece 36½ yards.
Black Galloon or Quality ſhoe binding —	0	2	0	the piece 32¼ yards.
Whited brown *Scotch* thread, Nᵒ 14, for the *Lancaſhire* cloth	0	3	2	*per* pound.
Ditto coarſer for the ſtays, Nᵒ 12, — —	0	2	10	Dᵒ
Coloured thread, Nᵒ 9, — — —	0	3	0	*per* pound.
Ditto finer, Nᵒ 16, — — —	0	4	0	Dᵒ
* *Scotch* thread, ſhort hanks, Nᵒ 8, — —	0	3	8	Dᵒ equal to 3 *d. per* ounce.
Ditto, — — Nᵒ 10, — —	0	4	4	Dᵒ Dᵒ 4 *d.* Dᵒ
Ditto, — — Nᵒ 16, — —	0	6	10	Dᵒ Dᵒ 6 *d.* Dᵒ
Ditto, — — Nᵒ 24, — —	0	12	6	Dᵒ Dᵒ 12 *d.* Dᵒ
Mancheſter tape for the petticoats — —	0	0	11	the piece 29 yards.
Ditto for Flannel Dᵒ — —	0	0	7½	Dᵒ 27 yards.
Holland tape, Nᵒ 13, for the Caps Nᵒ 1, and Nᵒ 2, —	0	0	3½	Dᵒ 18½ yards.
Ditto, Nᵒ 19, for the Tippets — —	0	0	4½	Dᵒ 19 yards.
Ditto, Nᵒ 27, for the Caps, Nᵒ 3, — —	0	0	6¼	Dᵒ Dᵒ Dᵒ
Striped tape for the Check Aprons — —	0	0	9	the piece 24 yards.
Shirt buttons, moulds, — — —	0	0	7	the groſs 12 dozen.
Coloured laces, round or flat, ell long, tagged at both ends,	0	2	10	Dᵒ Dᵒ
Hanover Lace, Nᵒ 2, for the Caps Nᵒ 2, and Nᵒ 3, —	0	1	0	the piece 9 yards.
Ditto Nᵒ 5, for the Caps Nᵒ 1, — —	0	1	4½	Dᵒ Dᵒ
Needles, common, Nᵒ 4, 5, 6, 7, mark 𝒟𝒽 — } Nᵒ 3, 4, 5, 6, mark Lo. Lo. C. — }	0	4	6	Twelve hundred.
Knitting Needles — — — —	0	1	0	{ *per* lb. containing 24 ſets, { 4 in each ſet.

* *N. B.* The beſt Thread is always ſtamped.

I N D E X.

H

INDEX.

INDEX

INDEX

Plate I

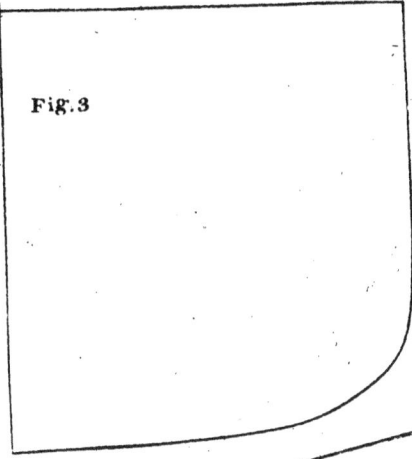

Fig. 3

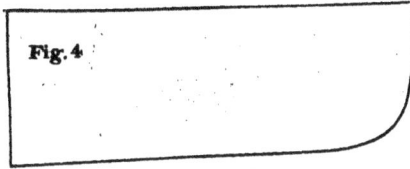

Fig. 4

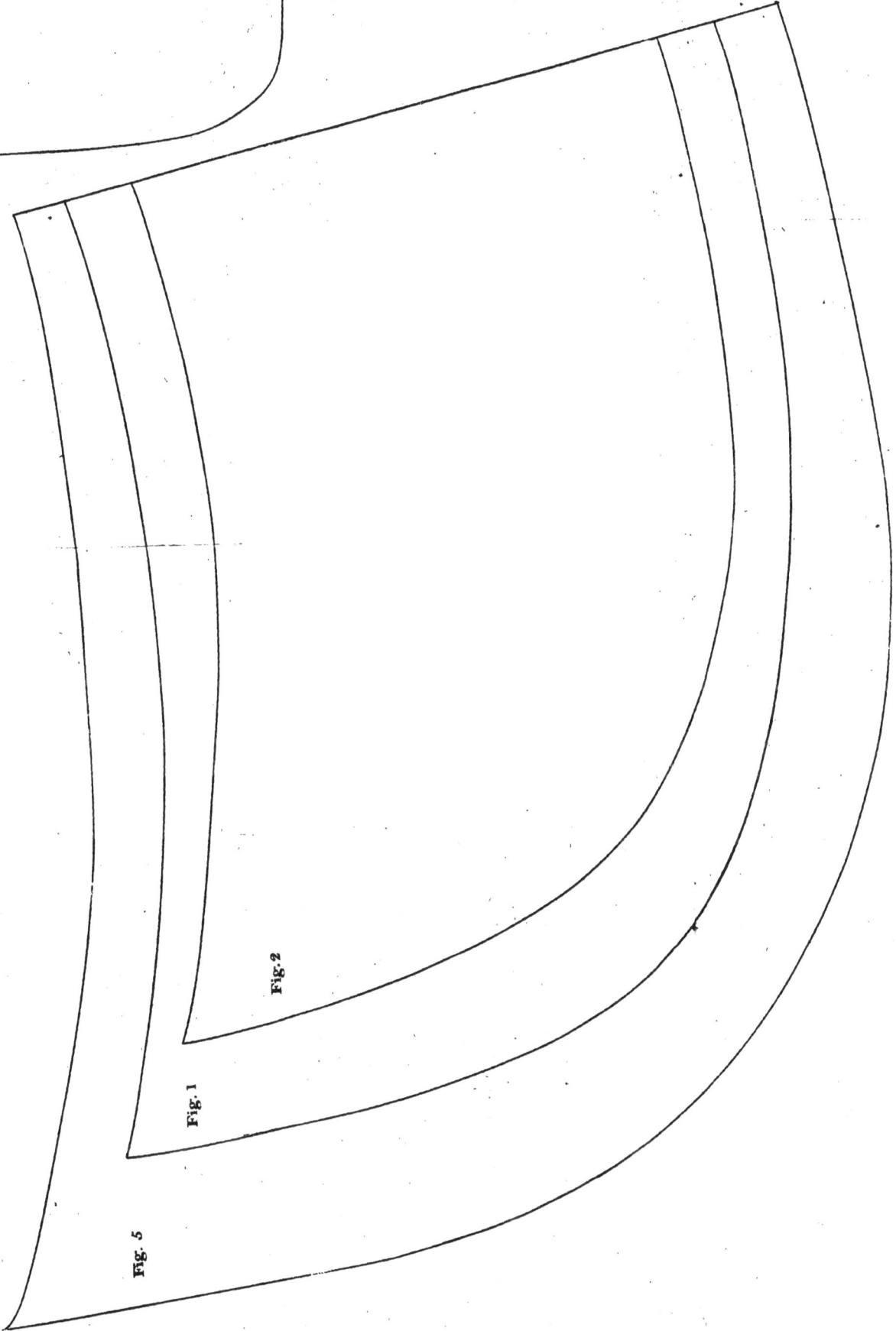

Fig. 2

Fig. 1

Fig. 5

Pl. II.

Fig. 4.

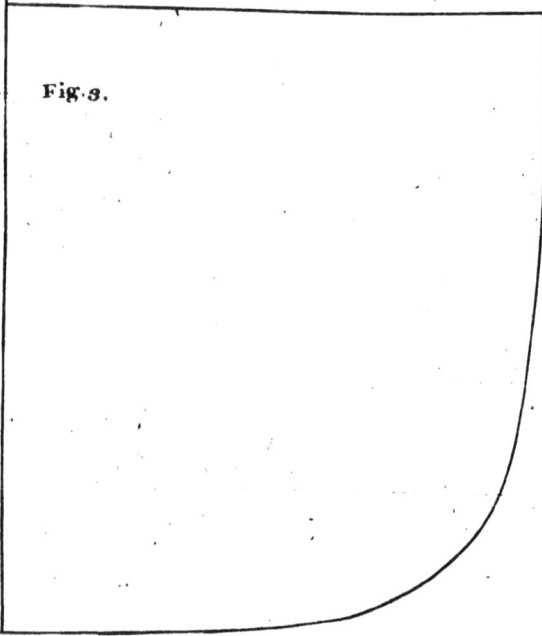

Fig. 3.

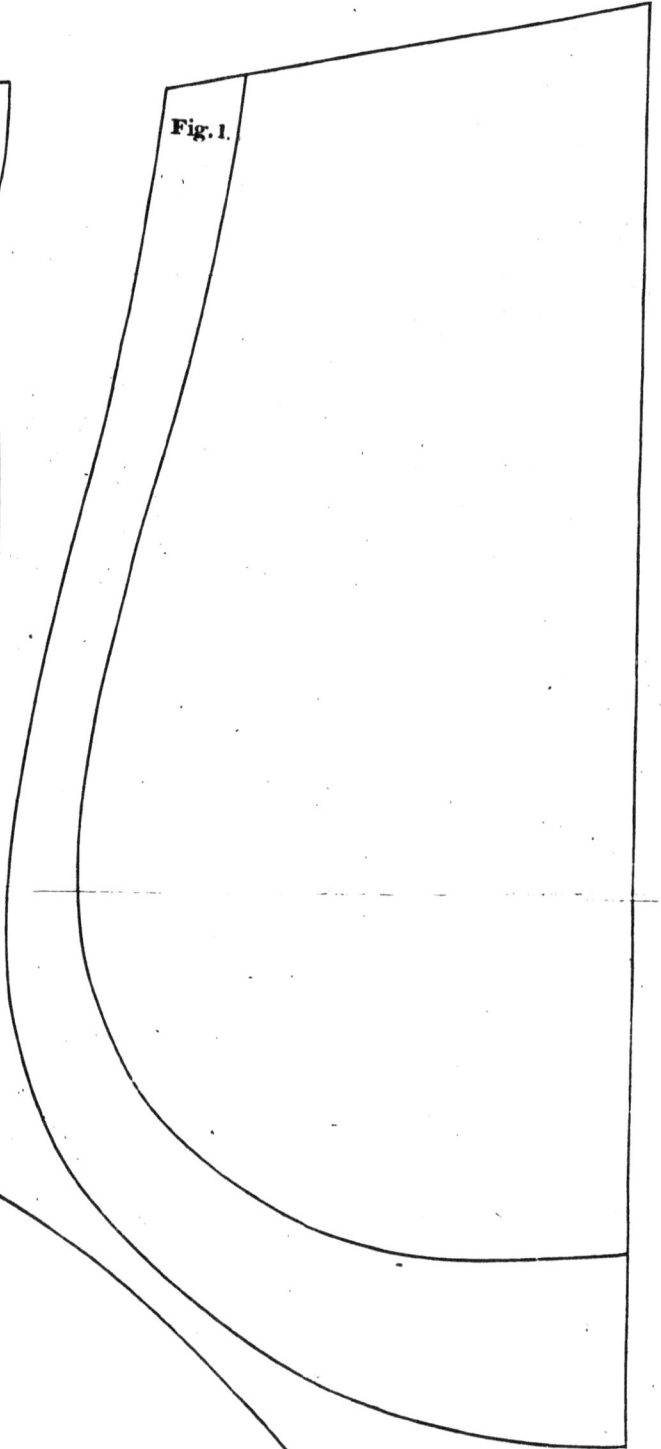

Fig. 1.

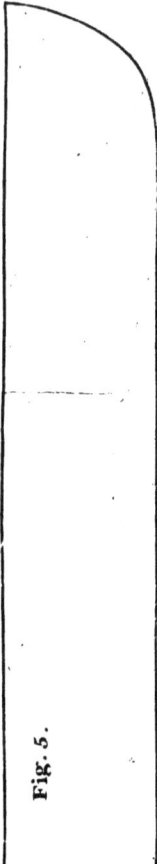

Fig. 5.

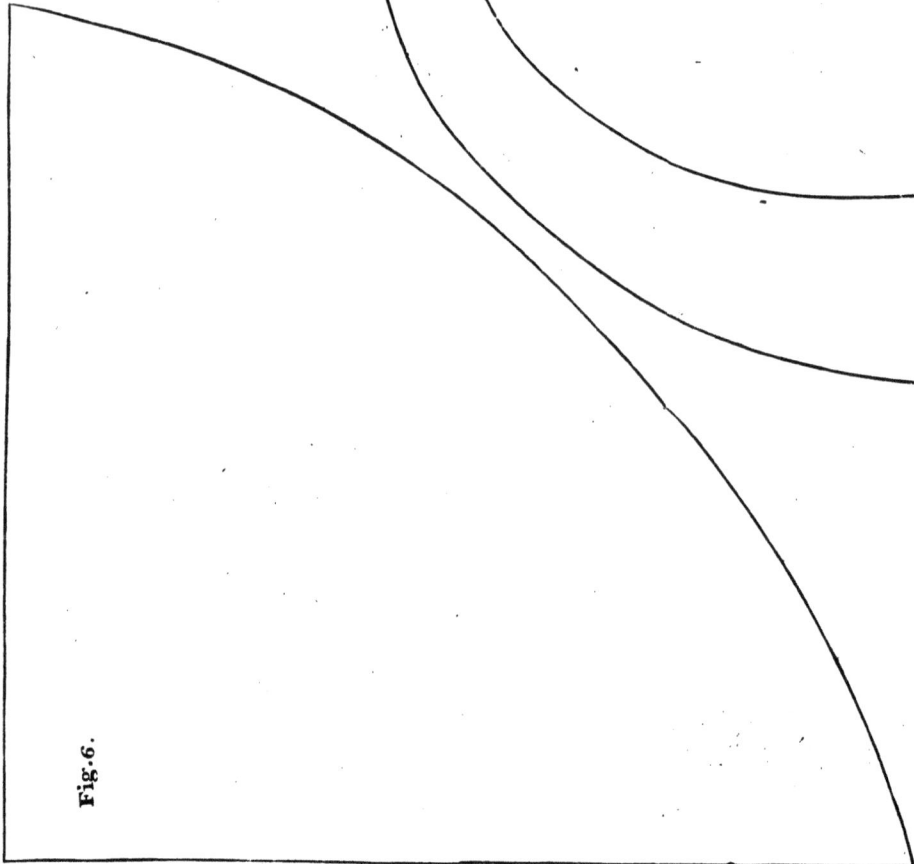

Fig. 6.

Fig. 4.

Fig. 1.

Fig. 2.

Fig. 3.

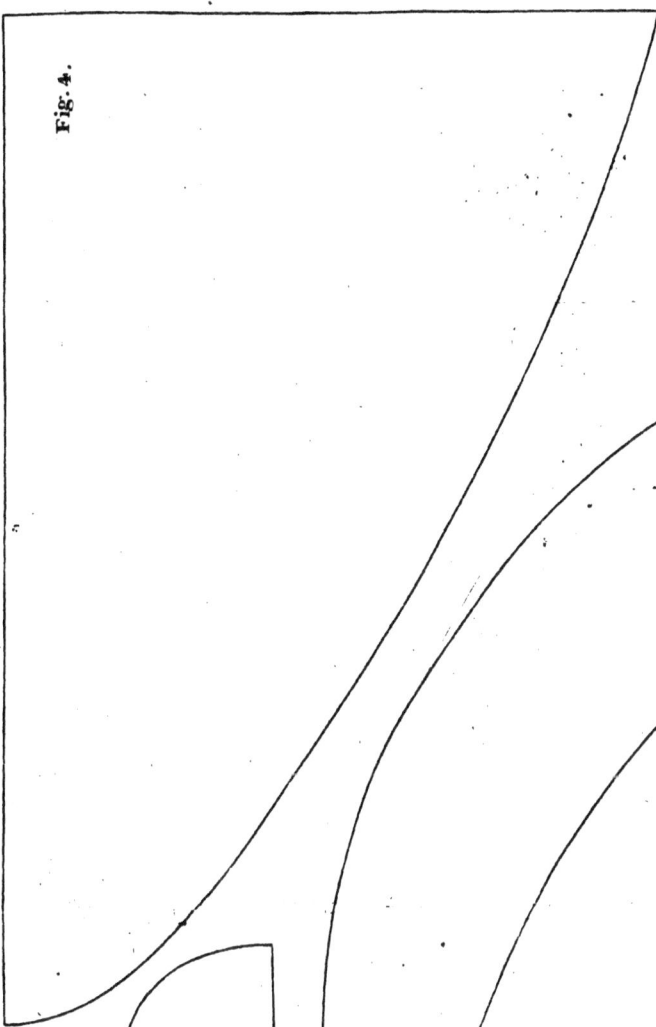
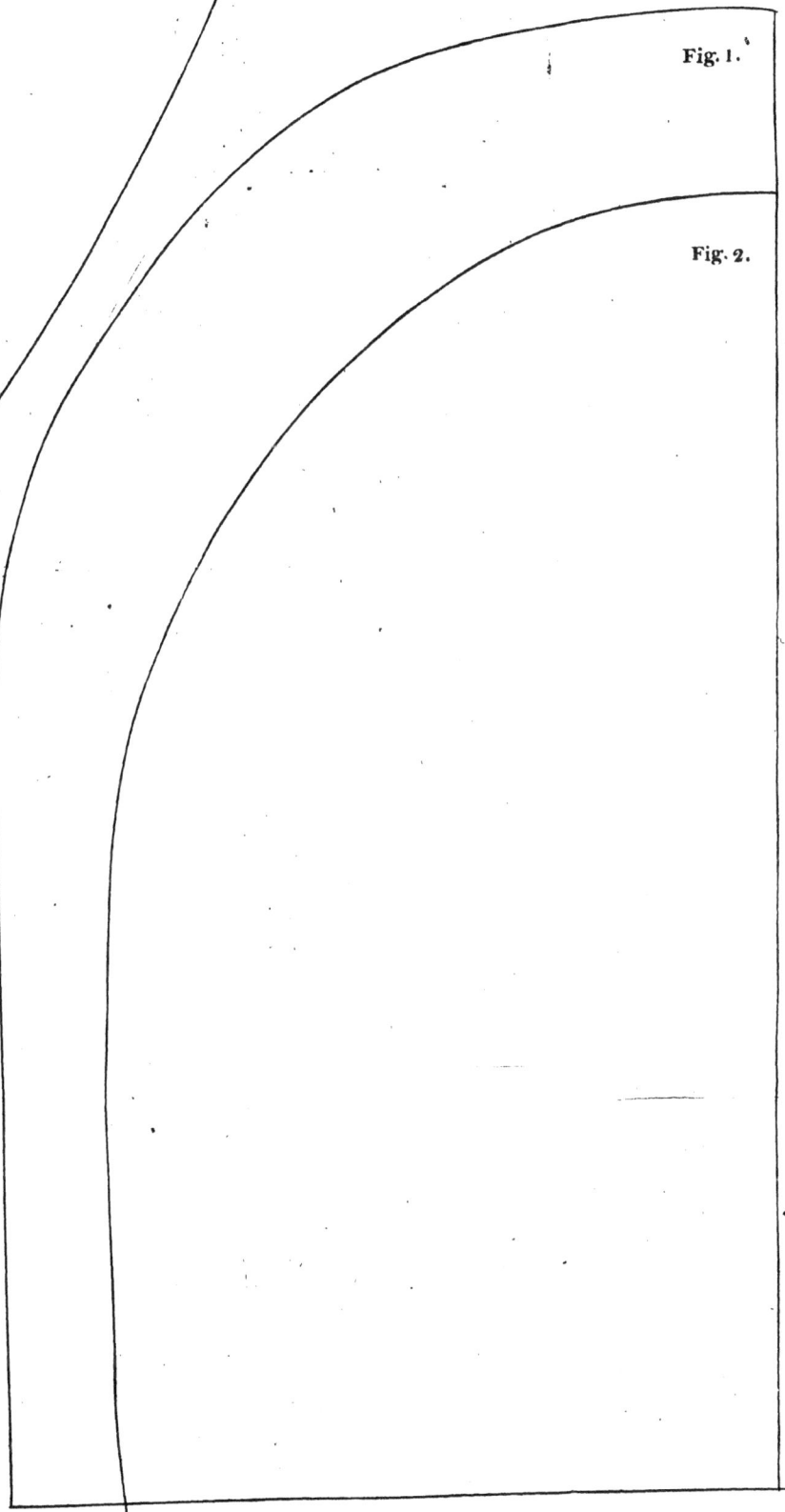
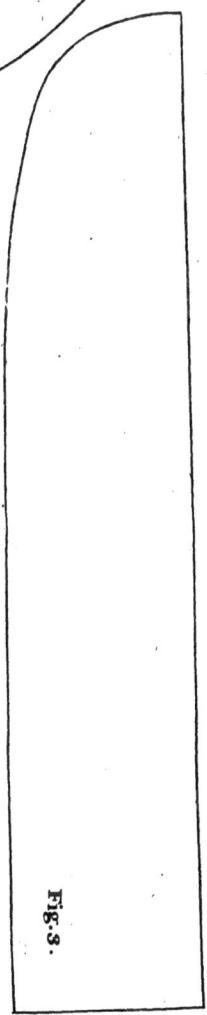

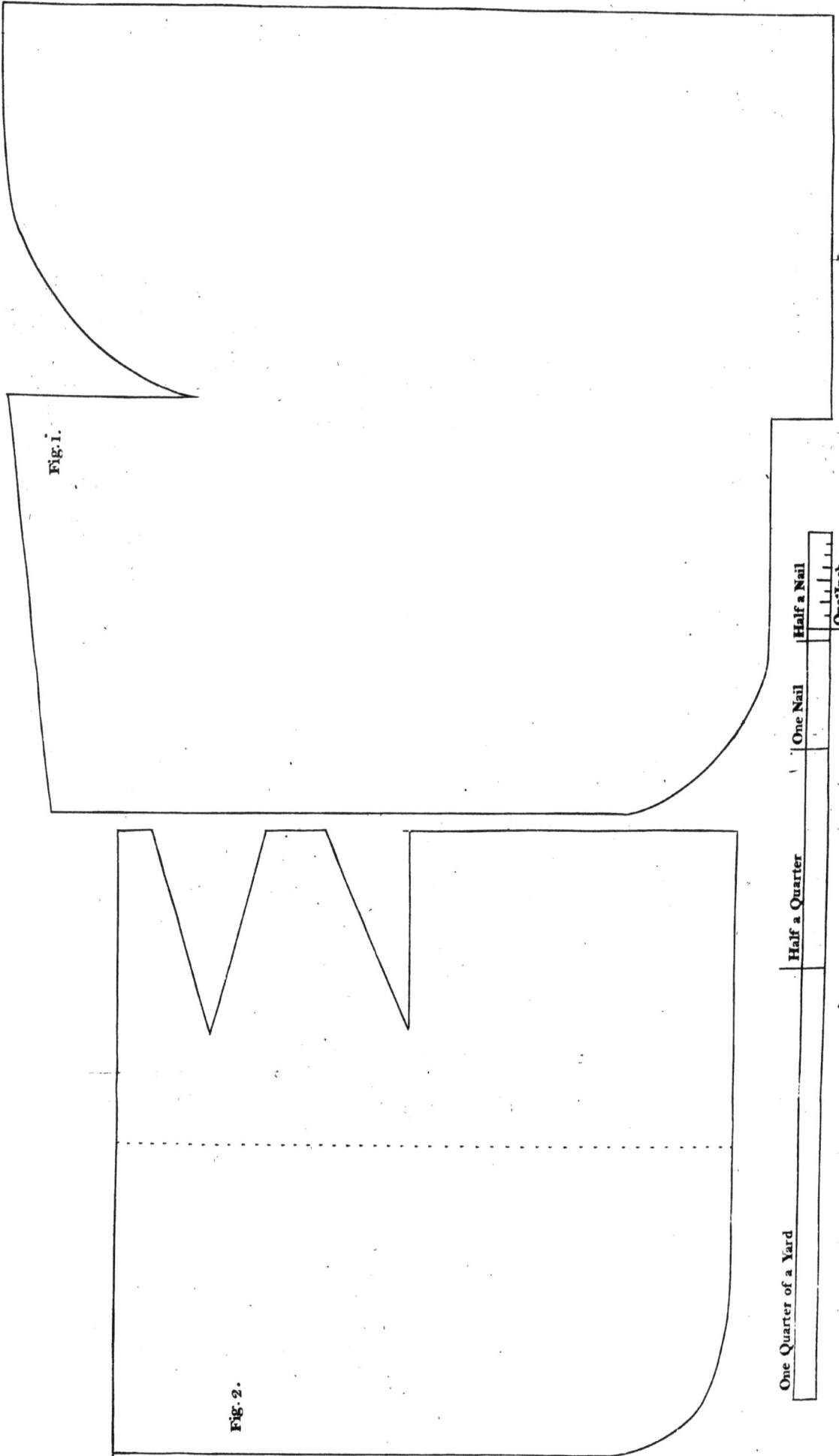

Pl. IV.

Fig. 1.

Fig. 2.

One Quarter of a Yard

Half a Quarter

One Nail

Half a Nail

One Inch

Fig. 1.

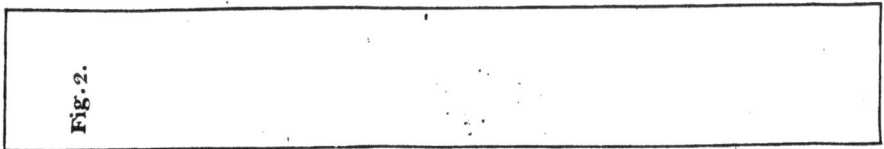

Fig. 2.

Pl. VI.

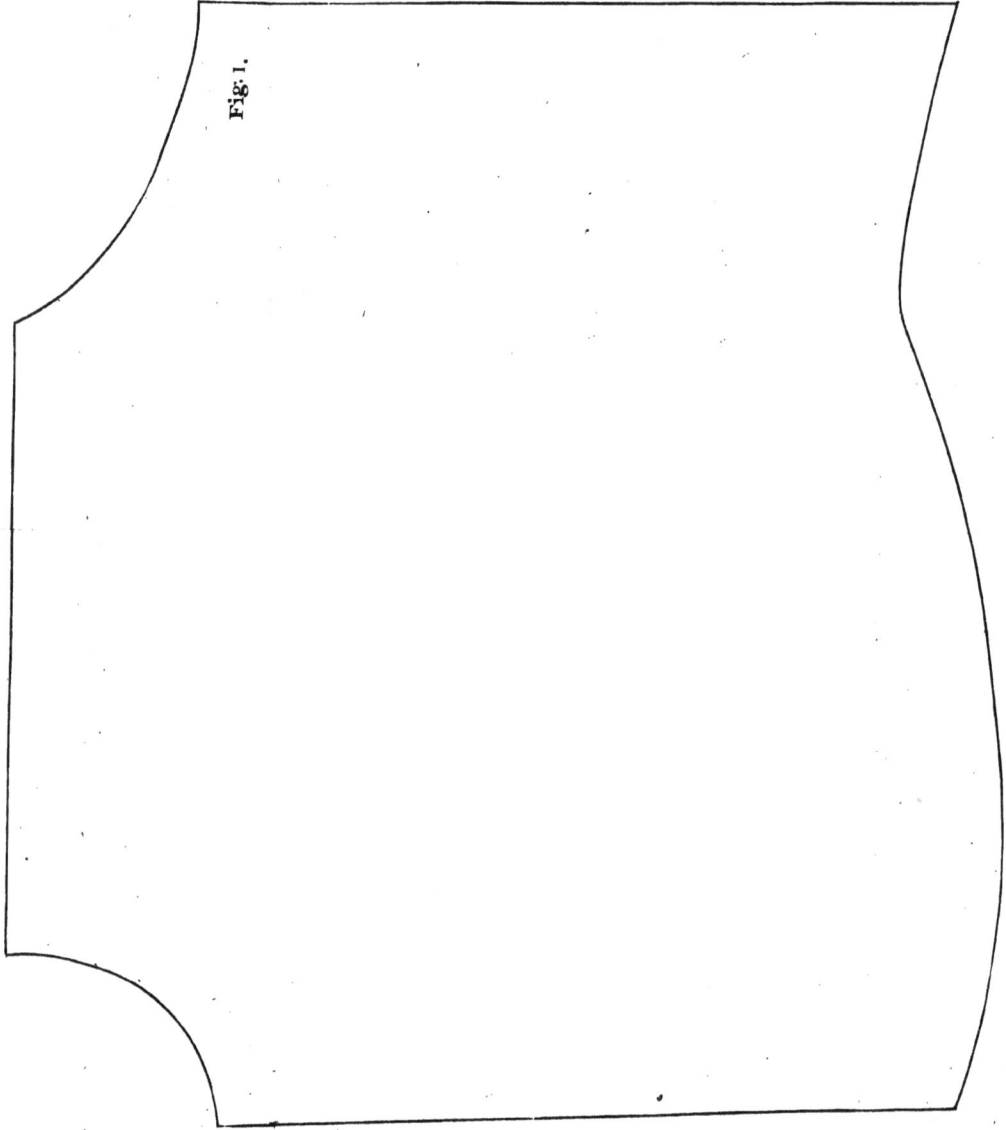

Fig. 1.

Fig. 2.

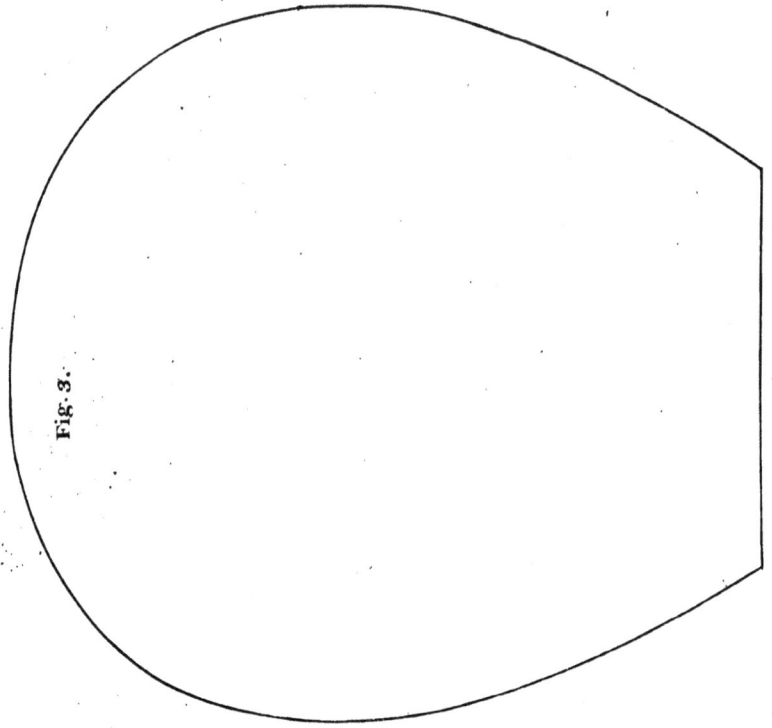

Fig. 3.

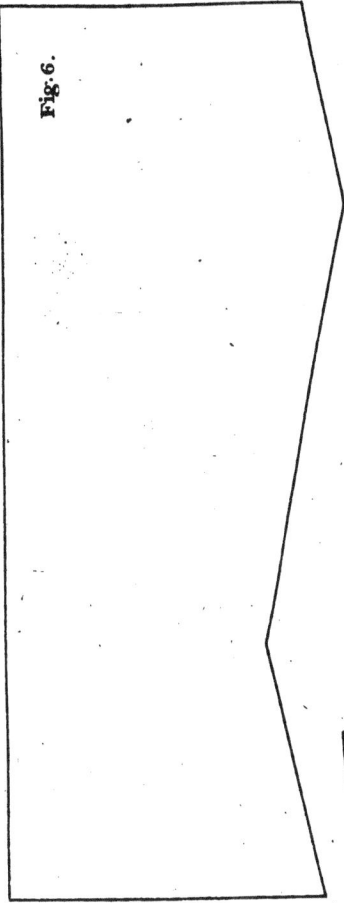

Fig. 6.

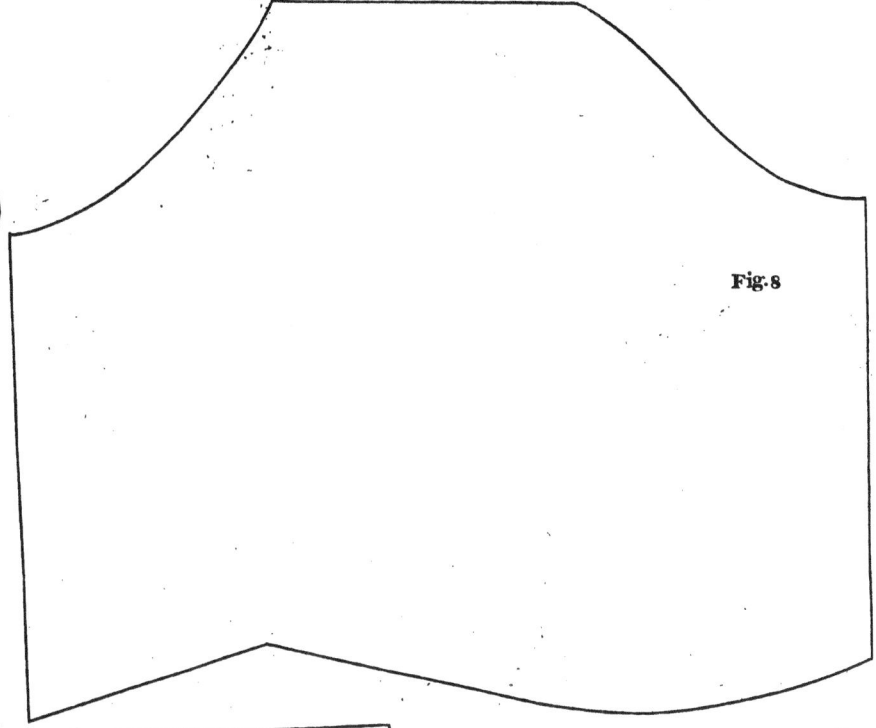

Fig. 8

Fig. 2.

Fig. 1.

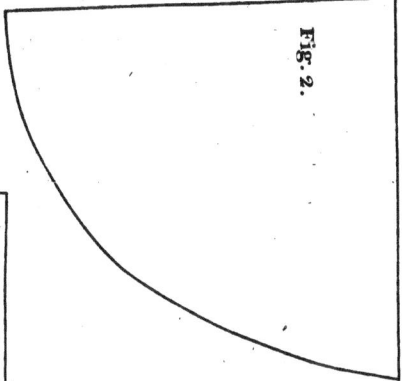

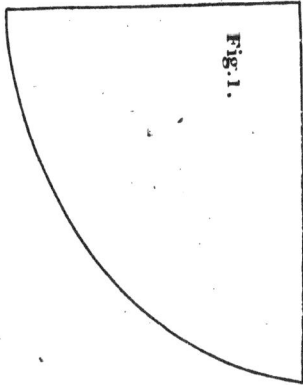

Fig. 7.

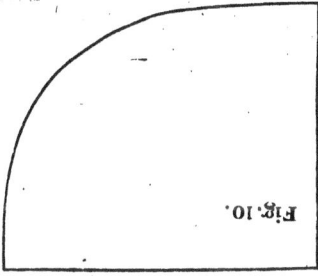

Fig. 10.

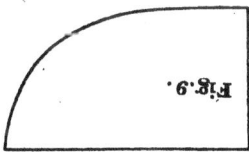

Fig. 9.

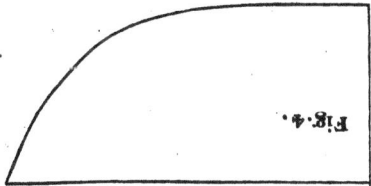

Fig. 4.

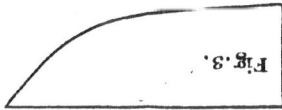

Fig. 3.

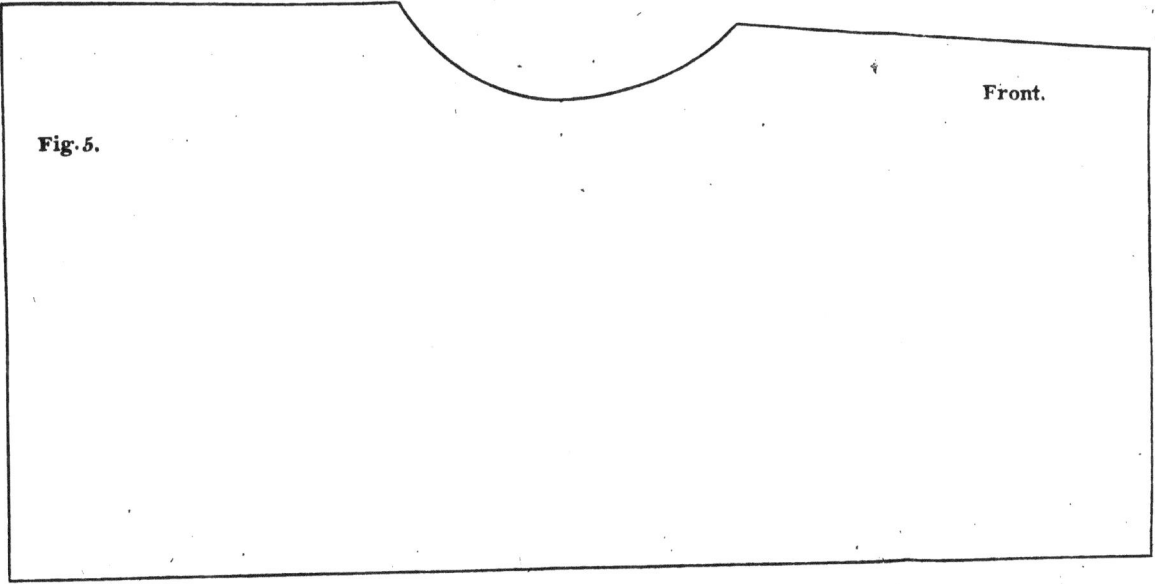

Front.

Fig. 5.

Pl. VIII

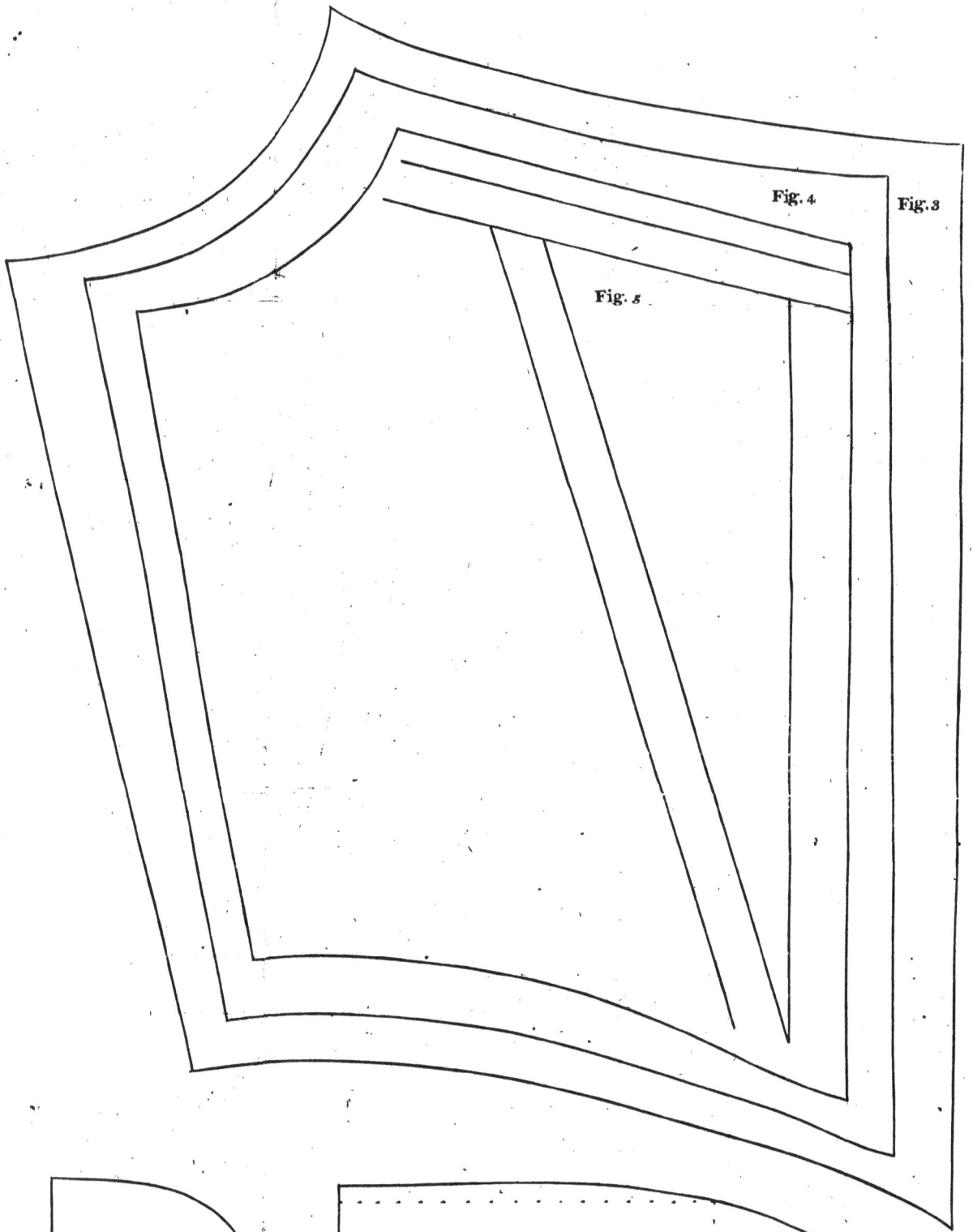

Fig. 4

Fig. 3

Fig. 5

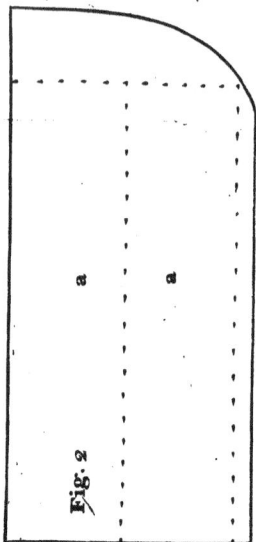

a

a

Fig. 2

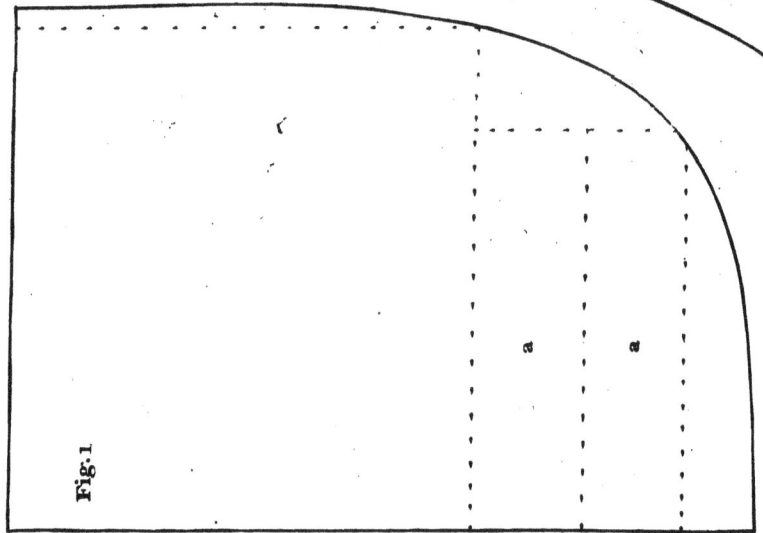

a

a

Fig. 1

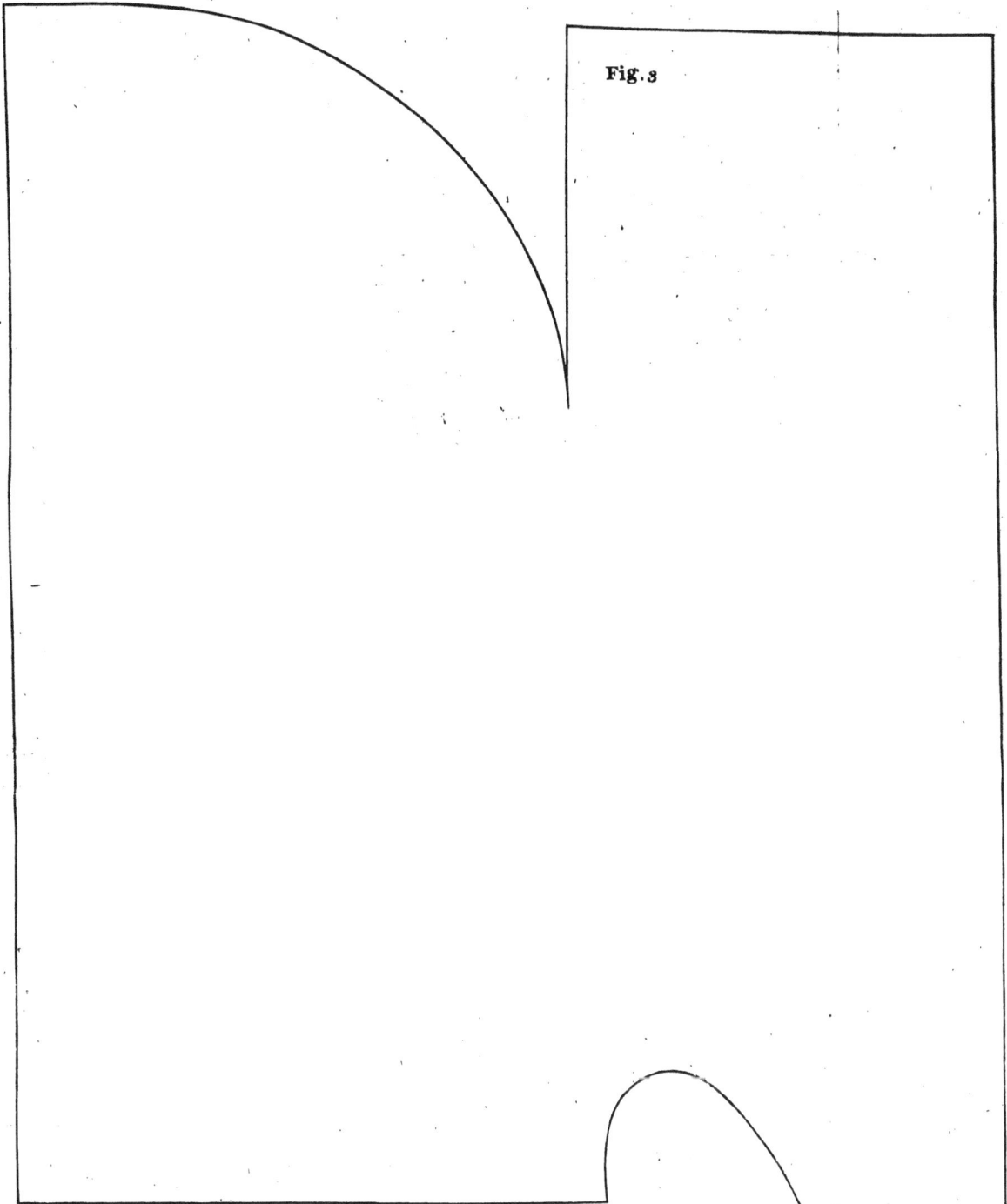

Fig. 3

Fig. 2

Fig. 1

Pl. X.

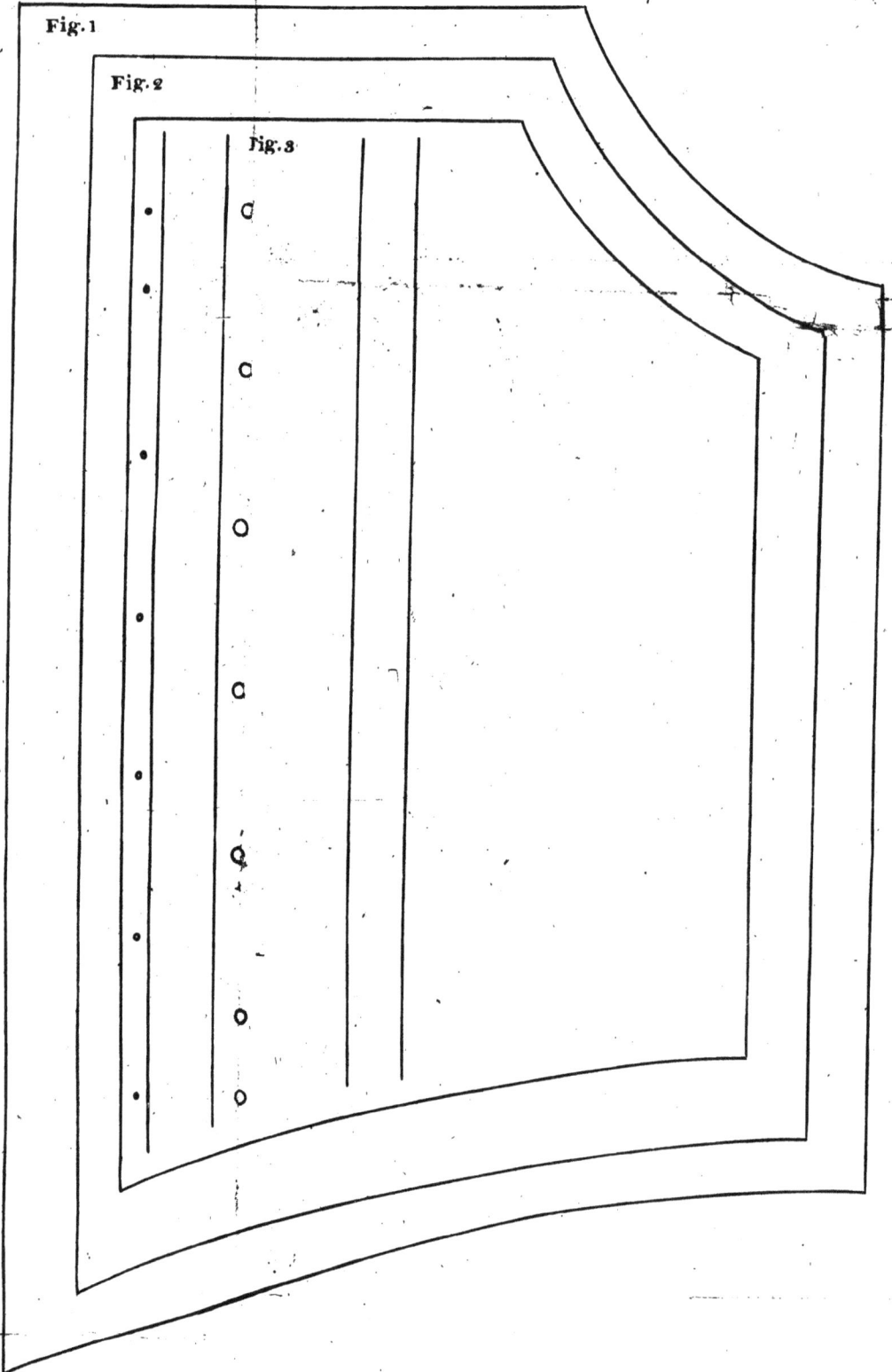

Fig. 1

Fig. 2

Fig. 3

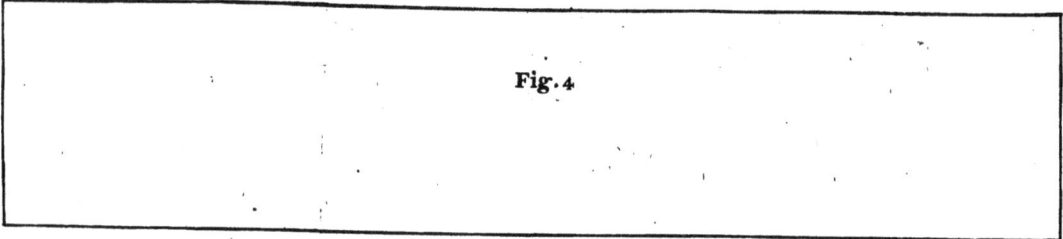

Fig. 4

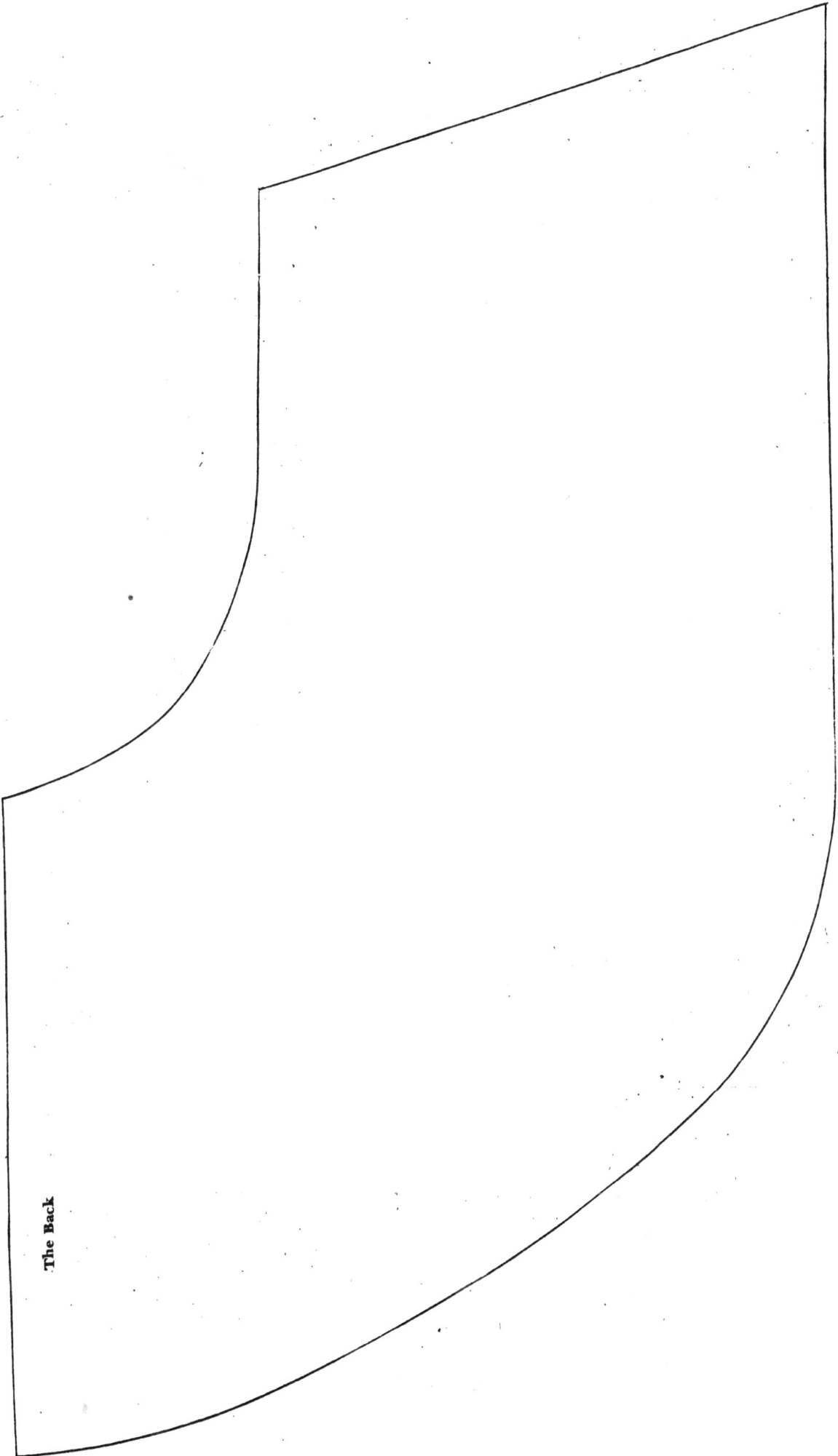

Pl. XI.

The Back

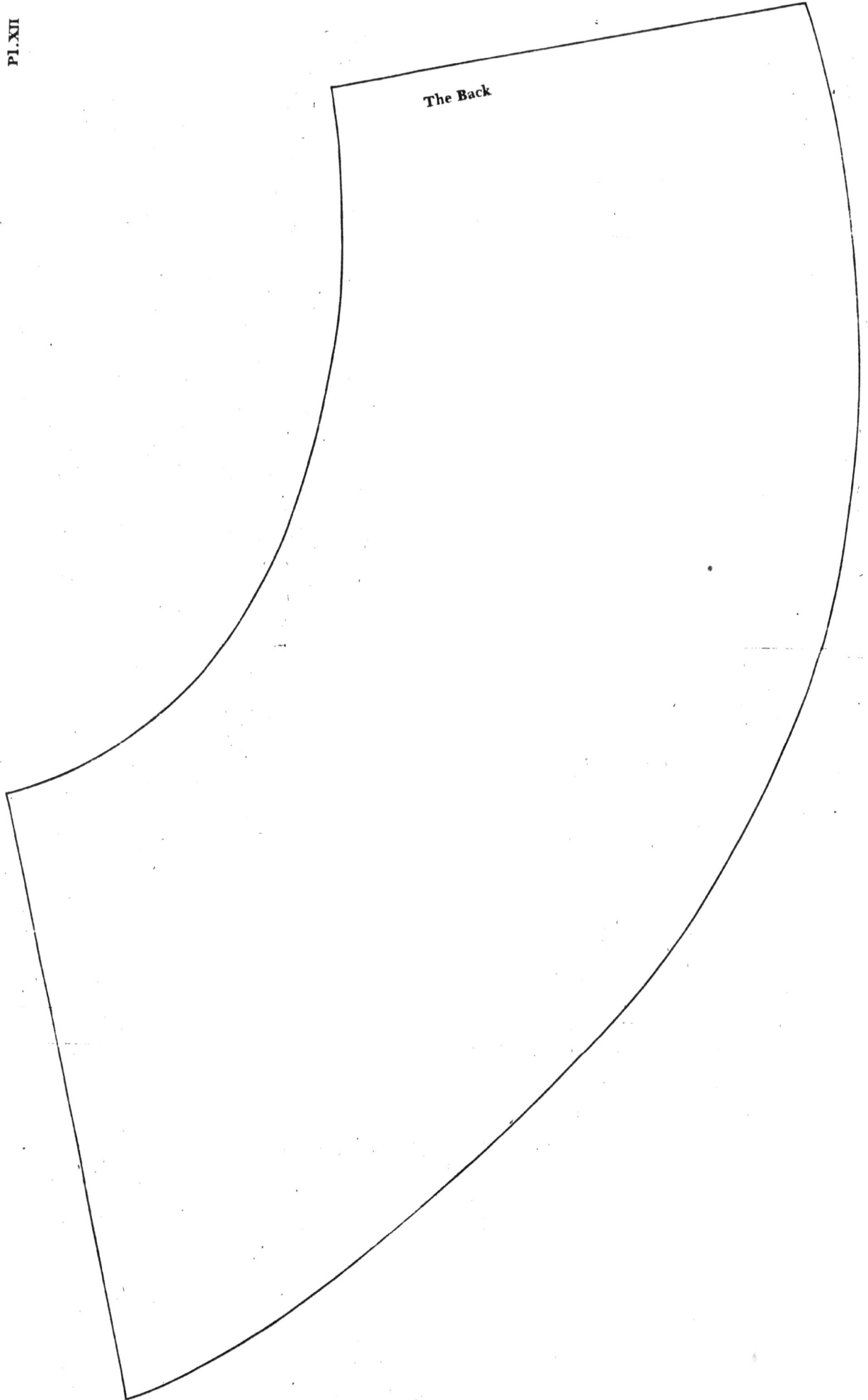

Pl. XII

The Back

The Back

Pl. XIII.

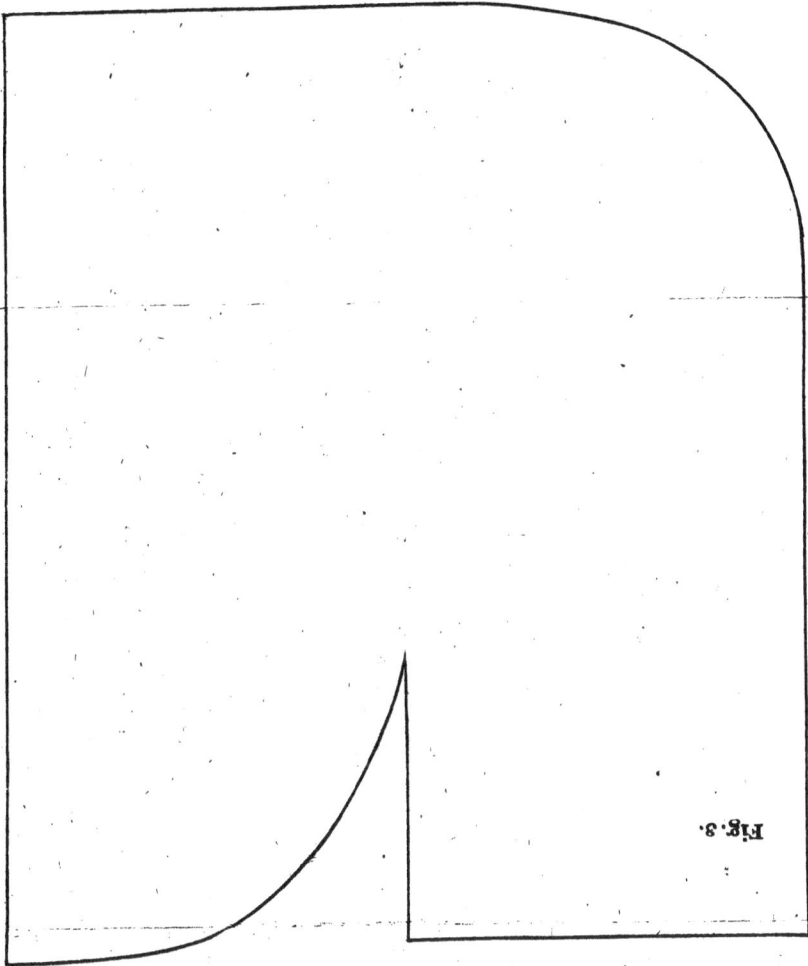

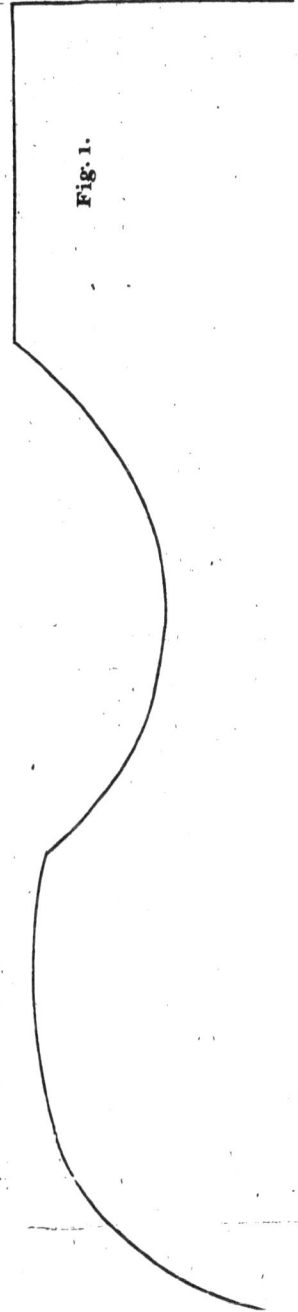

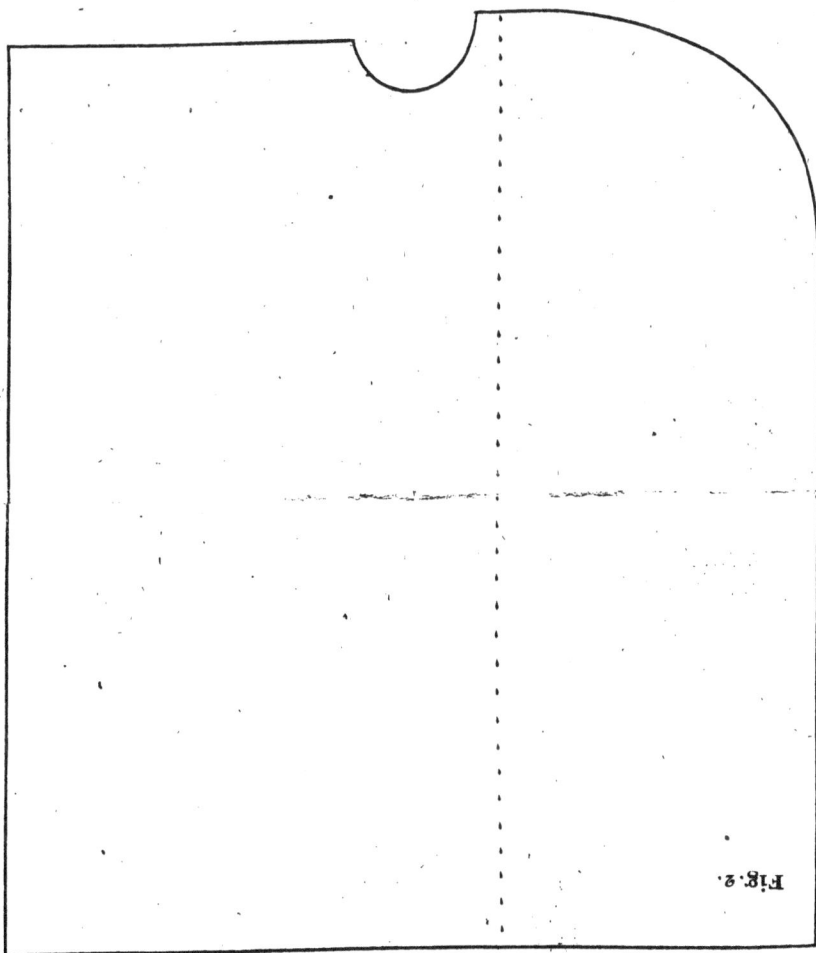

Fig. 1.

Fig. 2.

Fig. 3.